WHILE STROKING MY HAIR ... 'MUMMY I CAN SMELL MY BOTTOM ... ON MY HANDS ...'

SON: 'DID DINOSAURS DIE OF BOTTOM BURPS?' ME: 'ERR, I DON'T THINK SO WHY?' SON: 'WELL, HOW DID THEY GET STINKED (EXTINCT!) THEN?'

'MUMMY I'M GONNA HUG YOU SO HARD THAT YOUR EYEBALLS POP OUT AND THEN I'M GONNA EAT THEM!! SWEET DREAMS!!'

'MUMMY, DO POLAR BEARS POO OUT SNOWBALLS?'

GIVING US ALL DINOSAUR NAMES: 'MUMMY YOU ARE A BIT OF A DICKLIADOCUS'.

(ON FARTING) 'FIREWORKS OUT MY BUM!'

SINGING THE ALPHABET SONG 'A B C D E F G, H I J K L M N O P, CUCUMBER, T U V ...'

ANGELIC LOOKING DAUGHTER ON WAY TO HER FIRST DAY AT SCHOOL 'I HOPE THAT MY NEW TEACHERS TEACH ME HOW TO BE A VET. OR A SNIPER.'

I THINK MY WORST IS WHEN MY SON INFORMED THE WHOLE CAFE THAT 'MUMMY, THAT'S A MASSIVE COCK ON THE WALL.'

MY SON TELLS ME HE 'WUVS ME AS MUCH AS A SNAIL GOING ROUND THE WORLD A HUNDRED TIMES – BECAUSE SNAILS ARE SLOW AND THEY TAKE SO LONG TO GET ROUND THE WORLD HIS WUVS WILL NEVER RUN OUT' ... HE IS 6.

WHAT DO YOU FANCY FOR TEA? 'SKETTY BOLLOCKNAISE THANK YOU MUMMY.'

'DR WHO AND THE ONIONS ...' THE ONIONS?? 'ER ... OH NO I MEANT THE GARLICS. I'M SCARED OF THE GARLICS ...'

THE DAILY STRUGGLES

OF ARCHIE ADAMS

(AGED $2\frac{1}{4}$)

Also by Katie Kirby

Hurrah for Gin

THE DAILY STRUGGLES
OF ARCHIE ADAMS

(AGED 2¼)

KATIE KIRBY

CORONET

First published in Great Britain in 2017 by
Coronet An Imprint of Hodder & Stoughton
An Hachette UK company

4

A CIP catalogue record for this title is
available from the British Library

ISBN 9781473662025
eBook ISBN 9781473662018

Typeset in Consolas by Hewer Text UK Ltd, Edinburgh
Printed and bound by Clays Ltd, St Ives plc

Hodder & Stoughton policy is to use papers that are natural, renewable
and recyclable products and made from wood grown in sustainable
forests. The logging and manufacturing processes are expected to
conform to the environmental regulations of the country of origin.

Hodder & Stoughton Ltd
Carmelite House
50 Victoria Embankment
London EC4Y 0DZ

www.hodder.co.uk

To Mum and Dad for not selling me
to the circus when I was two.

I Can Draw!

The Daily Struggles

of Archie Adams
(aged 2¼)

PROLOGUE

Hello, my name is Archie and I start this diary on 25 February in a notebook I have been given to draw pictures of sunshines and flowers and farm animals in. Instead of doing those nice things I have decided to document my inner turmoil so that future generations of small people won't be so horrifically misunderstood.

You see there seems to be this new 'trend' of parents moaning about us on social media and I get so sick of hearing their one-sided discriminatory accounts! It's all . . .

 The kids have been such little arseholes today — bring on bedtime! #GinOClock #FML

 5   ♥ 17

I mean where do they get off speaking about us like that, are they forgetting we'll be choosing their nursing homes one day?

Anyway, before we begin, here are some fun facts you might like to know about me:

- Age . . . I am 2¼ years old – I know not much of this arbitrary thing called 'age', only that it is mostly used as a weapon against me and all the things I cannot do – use big-boy scissors, drive a car, drink beer, attend an all-night rave, etc.

- My family are . . . Mummy (highly strung, bit shouty, nice ears), Daddy (funny at times, bit pointless, good at farting) and Mr Fluffy the cat (moody, bit of a dick, stinks).

- I live in . . . A place called London, which is apparently one of the most expensive places in the entire world. Daddy refers to our house as 'the shithole' even though it cost about a twelvety billion pounds.

- Things that make me feel happy . . . Public nudity, mindless violence and Kinder Surprises.

- Things that make me feel sad . . . Broken snacks, the concept of sharing, and getting crap toys in aforementioned Kinder Surprises.

- Favourite foods . . . I am a strict follower of the trendy #BeigeFoodDiet.

- Least favourite foods . . . Vegetables (any), sauces (any), colourful foods (except sweets). Broccoli as a concept makes me very angry.

- Hobbies . . . iPad and telly.

- Favourite book . . . Toys R Us catalogue.

- Heroes . . . Chase from *Paw Patrol*.

- When I grow up I want to be . . . Chase from *Paw Patrol*.

- Five people (living or dead) I would invite to my fantasy dinner party . . . Chase from *Paw Patrol*, Father Christmas, Jesus, Darth Vader and Laa-Laa from *Teletubbies*.

SATURDAY, 25 FEBRUARY

I got up extra early today. I know this because
when I cheerfully shouted, 'MORNING, MUMMA!' she
responded with 'IT'S FOUR FUCKING THIRTY!', which
was pretty rude and uncalled for.

Apparently anything that starts with a 4 or 5 is
not a socially acceptable time to get up in the
morning . . . according to them! Works for me as I
get more iPad time because no one else seems to be
able to speak or function.

Is it bwekfast
time Mumma?

No. 4.30–6 a.m.
is YouTube time.

Later on Daddy went to the shops and came back with a thing called a Gro-Clock because they 'just can't take it any more!' It is supposed to be a fun game that involves not getting up until the sun comes on. Except it doesn't sound very fun.

Apparently tomorrow I'm to try really, really hard to win the game.

SUNDAY, 26 FEBRUARY

Tried really, really hard to wait for the sun but was ridiculously bored by 4.47 a.m.

I can't help being a morning person and I don't understand why other people seem to have such an issue with it?

Mummy looked tired and miserable all day. Probably drank too much Prosecco last night. I played her Beethoven's Fifth Symphony on my VTech Move and Groove music station to cheer her up.

Daddy said it was nice at first but was starting to get a bit irritating after two and a half hours. Ungrateful bastards.

TUESDAY, 28 FEBRUARY

I go to Little Angels Day Nursery three days a week, which is like an institution for poor neglected children whose parents don't love them any more.

While I am there, Mummy goes to work, where her job is to drink hot coffee and do 'important things' on a computer. I cry every time I get dropped off to make her feel like a career-obsessed bitch, but the joke's on her as I actually really like it. Am such a trickster – Ha ha!

My best friend at Little Angels is called Amelie The Magical Unicorn but as we are such good friends I'm allowed to call her Amelie for short. She wears a unicorn horn every day because that is what she is going to be when she grows up. She's nearly three and very sophisticated – she doesn't wear nappies any more and is learning to wipe her own bum.

Amelie hangs out with me because she feels sorry for me only being two and a quarter, and I hang out with her because she's dead clever and knows EVERYTHING!

WEDNESDAY, 1 MARCH

Today we had a 'You and Me Yoga!' class. I nailed my Modified Cobra and Noah cried because he can't even do the Downward Dog without falling over sideways. So pathetic.

Mummy resents the fact I do yoga, as apparently it's one of the reasons nursery is so ridiculously expensive. That and the fact that we eat organic free-range pineapples, do daily meditation and are learning to speak Mandarin.

Amelie reckons that pineapples should be free to wander wherever they choose and that Mummy should stop being so tight.

FRIDAY, 3 MARCH

Fridays and Mondays are AMDOF days, which stands for Archie and Mummy's Day of Fun because it's just us two and we can do whatever we like! Sometimes we go to playgroup, sometimes we go to the park, sometimes we go and make a complete spectacle of ourselves in Waitrose – the world is our lobster!

. . . although apparently it's hard to be enthusiastic when you've been up since 4.53 a.m. Spent the morning watching back-to-back episodes of *Paw Patrol* on Netflix while Mummy drank back-to-back cups of coffee while hunched over the Nespresso machine.

We had lunch on the sofa – a Pot Noodle for Mummy and a packet of Dairylea Lunchables for me – we are dead classy like that! Only ate the biscuits. Posted the cheese down the back of the radiator. Stored the ham in the back of Postman Pat's van in case of emergencies.

Said I was still hungry and she chucked a six-pack of Quavers at me. #WinningAtLife.

SATURDAY, 4 MARCH

Big day – learned how to get out of my cot!

Surprised Mummy and Daddy with this new development by appearing next to their faces and announcing I'd done a shit. They kept trying to put me back in bed so I think it may have been slightly before 7 a.m. Possibly 5 a.m.ish. Possibly earlier. Who cares?

SUNDAY, 5 MARCH

Daddy ordered me a big-boy bed so as I don't hurt myself when I repeatedly fling myself over the side of my cot.

Mummy asked him to Google if you could get a cage instead and laughed. Apparently there is a massive gap in the market for them. Mean.

All the benefits of a cage,
*whilst **definitely not** being a cage!*

MONDAY, 6 MARCH

Went out for a coffee with Mummy. It took seventeen minutes for my babyccino to arrive!

In the afternoon my big-boy bed got delivered and the big advantage of it is that I can get out of it really easily!

Amelie said that now I have a big-boy bed I get to decide when bedtime is.

Amelie said her record number of times for getting out of bed is 237. The challenge was on! Ate two bananas after dinner for extra energy.

9.23 p.m. Managed 254. Was knackered but pretty proud.

TUESDAY, 7 MARCH

They have got frustrated with my running around upstairs 'like a hamster on acid' so they have installed a stair gate on the door of my room.

I just lean over it and ask them questions until I'm tired.

Me: Can I have water, Mummy?

Mummy: Remember you hate water, darling!

Me: I lost teddy, Daddy!

Daddy: It's right next to your face, honey pie!

Me: I needs a poo!

Mummy: You've had three poos already today, cupcake!

Me: I love you Mummy!

Mummy: I love you my precious angel!

Me: I fink you are OK too, Daddy!

Daddy: Errrr . . . thank you, pumpkin!

Me: It too dark!

Mummy: That's because it's so late, beautiful!

Me: MONSTERS GONNA GET ME!

Mummy: There's no monsters, baby. Go to sleep now please!

Me: I not feel sleepy!

Daddy: GO TO SLEEP!

Me: OK, good night, Mummy!

Mummy: Good night!

Me: Good night, Daddy!

Daddy: Good night!

Me: What iz the chemical composition of magnesium?

Mummy/Daddy: *response unprintable*

I really enjoy this extra time we have together as it feels like we are really bonding.

WEDNESDAY, 8 MARCH

They thought they had finally won. They thought I was asleep. In actual fact I was just dismantling everything in my bedroom and making a big soupy pile of all my stuff in the middle of the room.

THURSDAY, 9 MARCH

The thieving bastards have removed all of my toys and most of the furniture from my room.

This must be what it is like to be in prison.

Amelie says it is an infringement of my basic human rights. #FML

FRIDAY, 10 MARCH

Mummy handed me a snack bar that she had 'accidentally' snapped in half this morning – I think you can guess what happened next.

Have made her a poster to stick to the fridge to avoid any further confusion on the issue.

Foods that should immediately
be placed in the bin...

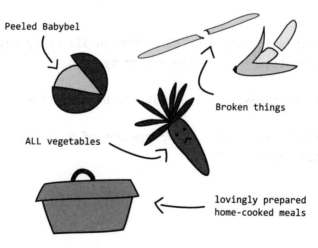

Peeled Babybel

Broken things

ALL vegetables

lovingly prepared
home-cooked meals

When Daddy came home he said if I could stay in my bed tonight and not get up until the sun comes up on my clock then I will get a special prize!

SATURDAY, 11 MARCH

Got fed up waiting and made a major discovery: if I randomly jab all of the buttons on the clock I can make the sun come up by myself!

Went to show them and Daddy lobbed it out of the window and called it a useless piece of shit.

So funny.

Later on I lobbed Mummy's phone out of the window, trying to hit one of those grey ducks of the sky.

Apparently that wasn't very funny?!

Her phone is broken now which means she might as well not exist as Facebook = life.

SUNDAY, 12 MARCH

Went into town so Mummy could try and get her phone fixed.

Apparently it's mangled beyond repair and the insurance won't cover it after I accidentally-on-purpose dropped it down the loo last time. #SoSad

Managed to convince them to take me to McDonald's for lunch via my best persuasion technique, the drop, scream and roll. Got a book in my Happy Meal and went absolutely ballistic again. Understandably.

MONDAY, 13 MARCH

Went to Tesco; always such a stressful experience.
So many wonderful products on offer, so many needs
left unfulfilled – I mean, how can they expect me
to be happy with bland, own-brand fromage frais
when there are Müller banana chocolate crunch
pots on offer? It's just bizarre. Had to have a
lie-down in the pet-food aisle to try and restore
my inner calm.

Mummy said that due to my 'recent behaviour issues' my Netflix privileges have now been withdrawn. No more *Paw Patrol* until I can learn how to behave. FFS.

TUESDAY, 14 MARCH

Today I will be demonstrating against my oppressed state by refusing to wear clothes. The demonstration shall last all day with complete disregard for anyone else's schedule.

THURSDAY, 16 MARCH

I have come up with a really lovely new routine:

4.45 a.m. – Start the day.

5.30 p.m. – Late-afternoon nap (usually timed to coincide with whatever monstrosity Mummy has put on the table for dinner).

6.30–9 p.m. – Generalised fuckwittery.

9.30 p.m. – Sleep.

Works really well for me!

Mummy on the other hand looks on the edge of a nervous breakdown, god love her.

FRIDAY, 17 MARCH

Had a tip-top day playing hide 'n' seek all afternoon. I always opt for my best place ... behind my hands! Clever, eh? It's so dark there, Mummy can never find me, the daft old bat!

SATURDAY, 18 MARCH

Mummy and Daddy were acting all shifty and then said they had 'something very exciting' to tell me.

Then they gave me a present. It was a bit small to be the Paw Patroller Deluxe Lorry but I opened it full of hope regardless.

Inside was a cheap-looking slogan T-shirt. They watched excitedly for my reaction, despite knowing full fucking well that I can't read yet.

I just felt livid about the Paw Patroller, if I'm honest.

Mental note: research pros and cons of siblings and reject proposal if necessary.

SUNDAY, 19 MARCH

The next day when I had calmed down (slightly)
about not getting the Paw Patroller, they
explained a bit more about the baby.

It is growing inside her tummy! I feel confused
and disgusted.

I asked some questions about how the baby got into
her tummy in the first place and they just kept
giggling and changing the subject. Very immature.

MONDAY, 20 MARCH

Did nothing today as Mummy was mostly being sick into the toilet. Poetry was my only solace.

'Can you even see me?'
A haiku by Archie Adams, aged 2¼

Beans on toast (again).
Left watching YouTube for hours.
Does anyone care?

TUESDAY, 21 MARCH

At circle time today at nursery my keyworker Jasmine announced to the group about the baby.

She said, 'GUESS. WHAT. EVERYBODY. ARCHIE. IS. GOING. TO. BE. A. BIG. BROTHER.' In a really slow, patronising voice and then made everyone clap. I was mortified.

Amelie had a little brother three weeks ago so she was able to reveal the intricate details of birth to us.

I vomited into my own mouth.

It gets worse – she also explained that when the baby is born it is going to live with us in our house . . . FOREVER! Apparently my mummy and daddy will forget about me completely and I will be like a ghost child that they ignore and only occasionally remember to feed.

THURSDAY, 23 MARCH

It's Mother's Day on Sunday so nursery provided
us with the banal task of making 'nice cards'.
They gave us pictures to decorate with feathers,
glitter and lots of brightly coloured paints.

I did mine all black to represent Mummy's fickle,
evil heart.

FRIDAY, 24 MARCH

Adults are literally always going on about healthy eating. Eat your poxy fruit and veg, too many crisps are bad for you, no more biscuits, etc. etc.

This is Mummy's diet at the moment: Ginger Nuts, salt and vinegar McCoy's and Mr Freeze ice pops. Smacks of hypocrisy!

SUNDAY, 26 MARCH - MOTHER'S DAY

Gave Mummy her card and she cried so I think she liked it.

Daddy took us out for a nice lunch but as I was still upset about the baby (and the fact I could see a microscopic fragment of carrot on my plate), I threw my dinner on the floor.

Mummy cried again.

Later on, as a special Mother's Day treat, I let Mummy go to the toilet alone, even though I'm not really sure she deserved it.

MONDAY, 27 MARCH

Went to playgroup today, not been in a while. I'm not a massive fan myself, the adults just sit around drinking coffee and looking like zombies while the kids have to sing stupid old-fashioned songs like 'Wind the Bobbin up'. I mean, come on – It's 2017, we are not stuck in the nineteenth century – get with the programme!

Why can't we have some Bruno Mars or Justin Timberlake?!

TUESDAY, 28 MARCH

Amelie said I need to make a stand as once the baby arrives there is no going back and having a little brother is the worst mistake she EVER made.

When I got home I rubbed Mummy's expensive make-up into the carpet. Not sure exactly how that was supposed to help but it felt quite therapeutic at the time.

Everything will be OK if I just keep on destroying things.

WEDNESDAY, 29 MARCH

Decided to start biting people.

Bit Sebastian because he was playing with the saucepan I wanted in the play-kitchen area.

Bit Ruby because she had a ridiculous bow in her hair.

Bit Archie Lewis because he has the same name as me and I hate being called 'Archie A' because it makes me sound unoriginal.

Bit Tom because . . . not sure. Just wanted to.

THURSDAY, 30 MARCH

Mummy and Daddy had to come in for an emergency meeting at nursery today to discuss my bitey ways.

Apparently it is a psychological response to the massive upheaval in my life caused by the baby news. I am feeling rejected and therefore I lash out at others for attention.

Sounds fair enough but I also just don't like people taking my things.

FRIDAY, 31 MARCH

Thought of the day – if biting is wrong, why does it feel so right?

Mummy says it's 'just not a very nice thing to do!' But if it's OK for football players and the clientele of Wetherspoons, then why isn't it OK for me?

SATURDAY, 1 APRIL

Had a lovely day spending some quality time with Daddy while Mummy had a well-deserved girly lunch. We played Lego, superheroes, had a fart-off competition and ate pizza in our pants (well I was in my pull-ups but details, details).

He said perhaps I might like to help name the baby and asked me what I might like to call it.

I have a very strong front-runner.

Later on when Mummy got home she seemed a little bit cross about the state of the house. I told her about our pizza pants party and she said Daddy ought to know better as he was nearly forty years old, not four! We giggled like naughty schoolchildren and did a secret high five when we thought she wasn't looking! I mean, who in their right mind doesn't like pizza pants parties?!

SUNDAY, 2 APRIL

Am feeling slightly better now about the arrival of Chase, so I have decided to temporarily stop biting. I wonder if it could actually be a dog instead of a baby? That would be my preference.

TUESDAY, 4 APRIL

Asked Amelie if mummies could have dog babies and she said she saw something like that on *Jeremy Kyle* once, so it's a high possibility.

Today's show: Worried I'm pregnant... with a dog!

WEDNESDAY, 5 APRIL

Keep having lovely dreams about me and Chase — we are going to be best buddies, I'm sure. I can take him for walks, play catch, feed him his Winalot, groom his beautiful long hair . . . I'm imagining he will be a Lassie dog or similar!

THURSDAY, 6 APRIL

I have decided that from tomorrow I will be eating all of my meals out of a bowl because I am a dog too. I will only speak in woofs and you must talk to me in woofs if you want me to answer you.

FRIDAY, 7 APRIL

5.02 a.m. Woof. Woof. Woof.

9.45 a.m. Woof. Woof. Woof. Woof. Woof. Woof.

3.27 p.m. . . .

Translation: Don't be idiotic — dogs don't wear shoes!

8.13 p.m. WOOOOOOOOOOOOOOOOOOOOOOOF!

SATURDAY, 8 APRIL

4.42 a.m. Woof. Woof. WOOOOOOOF!

Why is no one fucking responding?!

11.37 a.m. Bored of being a dog now. Am human again for the time being.

MONDAY, 10 APRIL

Some verse to share with you today . . .

Reflections on the buggy

A transportable straightjacket.

They strap us in and take us on journeys we have no desire to go on.

The post office, the supermarket, the chemist.

The supermarket, the chemist, the post office.

Will the errands never be completed?!

There is no means of escape.

Any resistance is met with a seemingly never-ending supply of rice cakes (PLAIN rice cakes).

The tasteless cardboard discs leave my mouth bitter and dry, yet still I continue to consume them – a truer paradox I never did find.

My fellow compatriots suffer a similar fate.
I lock eyes with them in Sainsbury's Local –
brainwashed, compliant, dead behind the eyes,
chomping on a lousy breadstick.

We sit dehydrated, forgotten, an irritation to
their busy schedules. Caged in a metaphorical
prison on wheels.

TUESDAY, 11 APRIL

I've discovered I am the exact same height as Mummy's vagina. My new game is to run at her and head-butt her in the foof. It is especially funny in public.

WEDNESDAY, 12 APRIL

11.33 p.m. Woke up in the night because my bones were feeling itchy so I went into Mummy and Daddy's room and found them naked doing unspeakable things!

I screamed and Daddy said they were 'just having a nice cuddle'.

Why would you do this naked, though? Why?! WHYYYY?!

Revolted.

WARNING:
The following page
contains graphic content

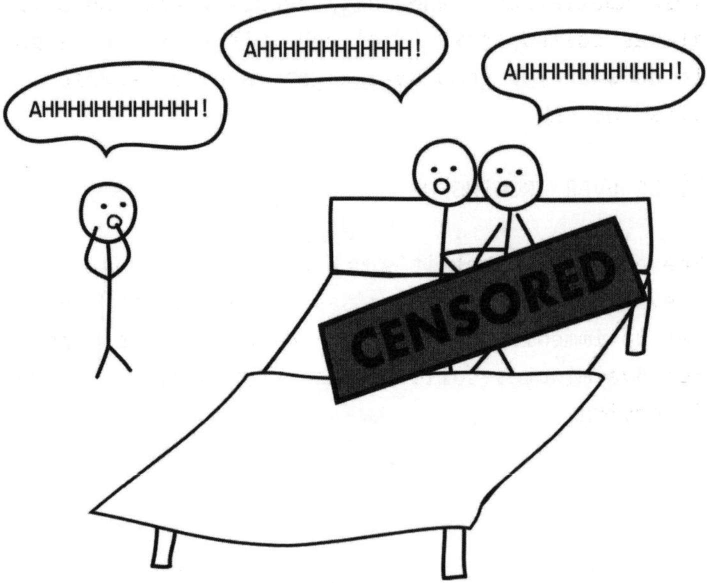
AHHHHHHHHHHHH!
AHHHHHHHHHHHH!
AHHHHHHHHHHHH!
CENSORED

THURSDAY, 13 APRIL

Told Amelie about the naked cuddling and she said it was called 'sexy time' and it's what you've got to do when you grow up and get married because it's THE LAW.

NEVER EVER GROWING UP!

She also said that it's how babies get made so if I ever hear any funny noises in the night I should get up immediately, go into their room and scream for five minutes solid and not stop until EVERYBODY is crying.

FRIDAY, 14 APRIL

Today is Good Friday, which is when we celebrate the horrific torture and murder of Jesus Christ by having a couple of days off work and drinking lots of beer. Cheers, Jesus!

Me and Mummy spent the day making crappy-looking spring chick cupcakes that she had seen on Pinterest. I don't really enjoy these types of activities and TBH I don't think Mummy does either – she gets stressed about the mess and the fact I can't distribute the batter evenly in the baking tray and I lose my shit because the cooking part takes too long . . . You know the score. But we do it anyway because apparently in order for Mummy to feel fulfilled in life she must validate her existence via Instagram likes.

You should check out her feed @mummylovesarchie – all absolute codswallop.

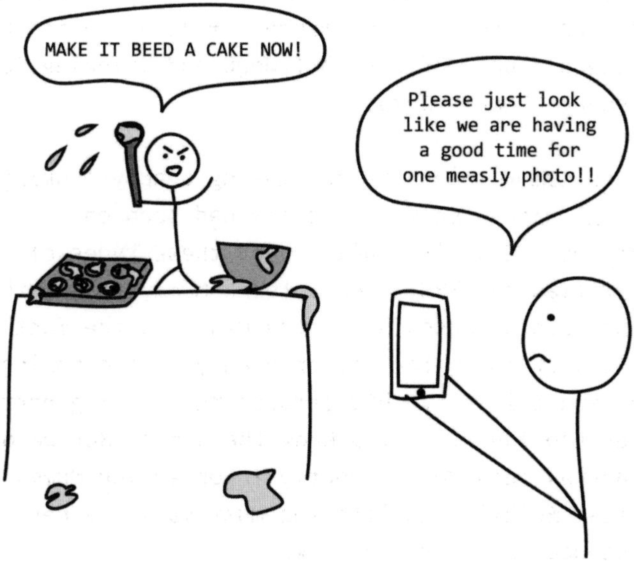
MAKE IT BEED A CAKE NOW!
Please just look like we are having a good time for one measly photo!!

SATURDAY, 15 APRIL

Mummy says that if I'm good a large rabbit will come to our house in the night and leave Easter eggs for us hidden around the garden.

Oh, what to think of this fucked-up life?!

Apparently it's something to do with Jesus being reborn but why Jesus coming alive again is celebrated via a chocolate egg-laying bunny is anyone's guess.

I just feel so dirty!

I am very dubious about the whole affair, to be honest – this is coupled with the fact that the cousins are coming. I do not care for the cousins. They look at my things, they touch my things and they want to do things that I do not enjoy to do. Sad face ☹

At least Granny is coming too – she is my favourite person in the whole entire world because she is not too busy to play with me and she refuses to listen to Mummy's slanderous accounts of my behaviour.

Just to warn you, he's been a bit ...

Oooh shhhh Mummy, I won't hear a word against my little cherub!

SUNDAY, 16 APRIL - EASTER DAY

Woke up. Ate chocolate. Ate more chocolate. Got tummy-ache. Vomited.

The cousins came. They looked at my things. They touched my things. They did things that I did not enjoy doing. They took part in the Easter-egg hunt, taking MY EGGS from MY GARDEN.

Granny came too. She likes the cousins, which only makes me hate them more.

We all sat down for a 'lovely lunch', which was actually disgusting. I decided to tell everybody about the naked cuddling which made everyone go really quiet and weird.

Everything started to get a bit much for me in the afternoon. I was overcome by a sea of rage and I started throwing stuff and screaming. Apparently Jesus would not have approved of such ungrateful behaviour. Bothered.

Anyway, I was glad when everyone left and I was alone with my chocolate.

P.S. Special shout-out to Cadbury for sponsoring Jesus's resurrection and making it so delicious. He must've been hungry after he came out of his cave and I'd like to think he enjoyed a good few Creme Eggs and a Double Decker.

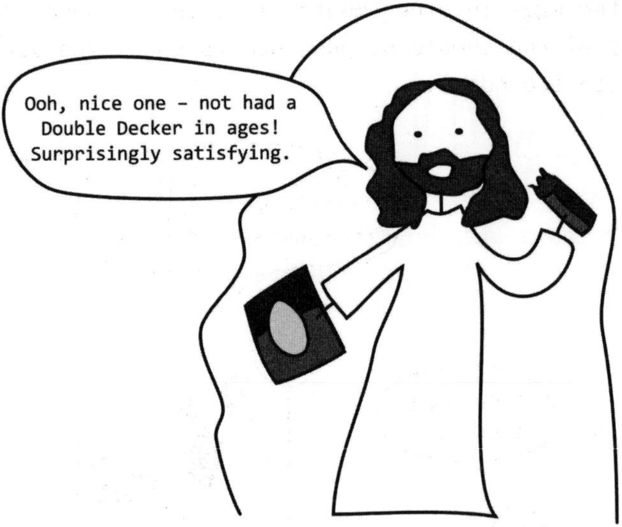
Ooh, nice one - not had a Double Decker in ages! Surprisingly satisfying.

MONDAY, 17 APRIL

Found Mummy hiding in the kitchen, stuffing my Easter eggs into her mouth. It's theft, pure and simple! And should be punished as such. The dirty rotten scoundrel!

TUESDAY, 18 APRIL

Bumped into our next-door neighbour Lucy on the way back from nursery and it turns out she is pregnant too and her baby is due around the same time. Joy.

I dislike Lucy as she gives Mummy disapproving looks when I am expressing my individuality on the driveway. Also she is a passive-aggressive, know-it-all bitch.

FRIDAY, 21 APRIL

This morning Mummy announced that we were having 'friends' over for a 'playdate'.

I'm well aware that those words make the events that were about to transpire sound considerably more appealing than they actually were, so for those who may come into contact with this diary in years to come, **please proceed with caution**. These are some things that I have learned the hard way:

1. 'Auntie [insert name of other parent]' will not be an actual auntie, just one of your Mummy's boozehound waster friends.

2. The child they come with will be an irritating, snotty-nosed blathering idiot.

3. The adults (AKA dirty perverts) will ignore you completely and talk about people they fancy off CBeebies. FYI, Mummy – Mr Bloom is not that hot, you're just getting old and desperate!

4. Occasionally they will shout stuff like 'Play nicely now!' and 'Share!' EVEN WHEN YOU ARE ACCIDENTALLY-ON-PURPOSE HIT IN THE FACE WITH YOUR OWN FIRE ENGINE.

5. Then when you legitimately retaliate by attempting to stab the snotty-nosed blathering idiot in the eye with a screwdriver (that you managed to obtain due to improper supervision – see point 3) you will be sent to sit on the naughty step while the other child is given one of YOUR Bourbons.

6. In conclusion: you should consider legal action against any parent using the term 'playdate', as it is a serious breach of the Trade Descriptions Act 1968. A more accurate term would be 'pre-organised violation of one's home, possessions and physical self'.

SUNDAY, 23 APRIL

I'm dying. I'm literally dying. Such is the pain that all I can do is writhe around the floor and scream. I practically OD'd on a bottle of Calpol by mid-arvo.

Apparently I have a new molar coming and it is 'just a tooth and nothing to be so upset about'. Tsk tsk.

I suffer, we all suffer.

WEDNESDAY, 26 APRIL

Wash your hands, brush your teeth, stop playing with your willy, don't run into oncoming traffic, look where you are going, don't hit people, stop trying to ride Mr Fluffy – it's like living under a dictatorship!

THURSDAY, 27 APRIL

Mummy usually picks me up from nursery at 5.30 p.m. and it is my favourite time of day (but shhhh, don't tell anyone). Every time the doorbell rings my heart skips a beat and I always feel so sad if it isn't her. And then when it finally is, she makes the whole playroom light up with her smile and I feel like I am about to POP LIKE A BALLOON FULL OF HAPPINESS! I don't know who decided that she would be my mummy but I know I have the best one ever.

Anyway, today she arrived at 5.32 and it was the longest two minutes of my life ☹ – especially as I had made her an extra-special sculpture that I knew she would love!

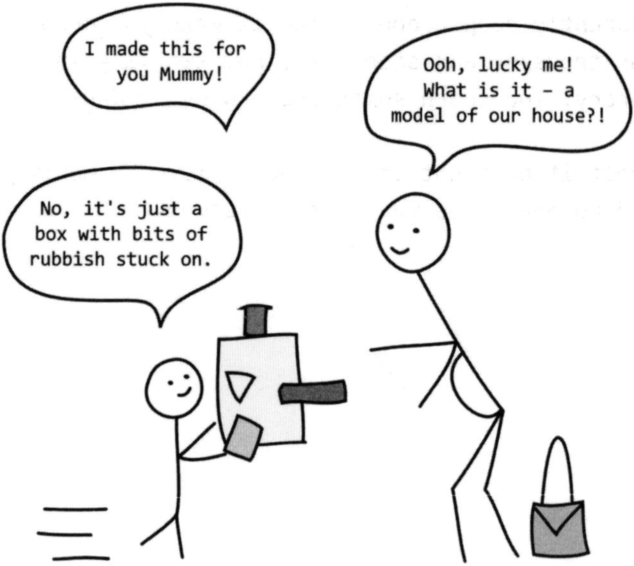
I made this for you Mummy!
Ooh, lucky me! What is it – a model of our house?!
No, it's just a box with bits of rubbish stuck on.

SATURDAY, 29 APRIL

Apparently people don't like it when you drop your trousers and start bare bum twerking in the library. You learn something new every day!

I felt it best not to include a picture. Mummy said no one needs to see that again.

MONDAY, 1 MAY

Today is a bank holiday so they came up with the ludicrous notion of going to Ikea along with every other twat in the country.

First we had meatballs for lunch, which I refused to eat on principle – I mean who eats meatballs and jam – who?! Apparently 'everyone loves them' but I don't care, I shan't conform to these ridiculous societal norms just to fit in.

Next Mummy tried to leave me in the crèche by pretending I was three, but I told them I was two so they refused to take me. In her face!

Then we went on an incredibly bizarre journey through a sequence of other people's living rooms and kitchens while Daddy intermittently shouted out stuff like 'We do not need any more of those!' 'We only came to buy a cot!' 'Stop jumping on the beds!' 'I don't care if it's only £3, we have enough bastard throws!' 'I hate candles!' 'Get out of the wardrobe!' 'I hate pillows!' 'I do not have an opinion on spatulas!' 'Get off it!' 'Get down!' 'Get up!' 'Why are you buying him a circus tent?! Where the hell are you going to put the circus tent?!!' and 'I will fucking leave you if you buy any more tea lights!'

Finally they had a massive barney in the self-serve section because Daddy had written down the wrong aisle number for a shoe rack they didn't even need and by the time we left, and had spent twenty-five minutes trying to jam everything in the car before taking it back into the shop and paying for home delivery service because it wouldn't fit, they were on the brink of divorce – which apparently was just part and parcel of a trip to Ikea on a bank holiday weekend.

What a lovely day!

TUESDAY, 2 MAY

I have just found my sculpture *Box with Bits of Rubbish Stuck on* shoved unceremoniously into the recycling bin alongside *Sammy the (Toilet Roll) Snake*, *Gustav the Space Hedgehog* (incorporating the medium of pine cone, avec glitter and googly eyes) and an insultingly large wodge of my favourite paintings, including the popular 'Potato-printing series XVI', versions 27–84.

I confronted the two key suspects – a shifty-looking middle-aged couple, who reside on the premises of the crime scene – and both denied any knowledge of the incident, insisting it must have been 'an accident'.

Outcome:

- Insist all works of art are clearly and prominently displayed.

- Keep a detailed log of all pieces brought home and conduct regular spot-checks to ensure nothing is missing.

- Closely monitor contents of recycling boxes and bins until trust levels have been restored.

- Look into costs of installing CCTV to catch the perpetrators in action.

- Do not let the philistines crush your creative spirit. Their inability to understand the depths of your talent stems from a lowbrow and uncultured upbringing.

WEDNESDAY, 3 MAY

Daddy has just told me that as a special treat next Monday I get to come to the hospital with them to see the baby puppy. They can do a magic trick so you can see the insides of Mummy's tummy on a TV. Sounds gross but at least I'll get to see Chase. I wonder if she has the whole of Adventure Bay inside her tummy too?

THURSDAY, 4 MAY

Can't wait to meet Chase!

FRIDAY, 5 MAY

Can't wait to meet Chase – why is it taking forever?!

SATURDAY, 6 MAY

STILL NOT THE DAY I GET TO MEET CHASE!!!!

SUNDAY, 7 MAY

TOMORROW WE GET TO MEET CHASE FOR THE FIRST TIME EVER.

MONDAY, 8 MAY

4.34 a.m. Woke up and bounced out of bed with a real spring in my step because TODAY IS THE DAY I GET TO MEET CHASE! AM SO EXCITED I CAN HARDLY EVEN BREATHE! The appointment is not until 9.30 a.m. How the hell will we fill the time?!

8.47 a.m. We are finally off to the hospital. Mummy has been feeling quite nervous so I have spent the last few hours doing chores around the house. Not everyone has been as grateful as I had envisaged. How was I to know that the DVD player doesn't like eating jam toast?!

You look hungry Mr DVD!

Will update as soon as we get back!

11.30 a.m. Home again. I don't want to go into full details as I am too upset, but that was an utter disaster and we are no longer on speaking terms. There is no puppy. It is a baby. Absolutely devastated.

TUESDAY, 9 MAY

Told Amelie about Chase not being a dog. She said scans are not entirely accurate and they can sometimes get these things wrong. All is not lost.

WEDNESDAY, 10 MAY

They set up a shaving-foam tray today at nursery. I watched in distaste as the mindless idiots shrieked in delight and rubbed it into their hair. Jasper, as usual, tried to eat it.

Sigh. Why is life so bleak?

FRIDAY, 12 MAY

I love going on the swings at the park; they are often so therapeutic for my troubled mind. Sometimes I think I could stay on for hours – sometimes I do stay on for hours.

The only problem is that Mummy doesn't seem to share my love of swings and every visit ends in an inevitable stand-off:

Mummy: I think it's nearly time to go home now, Archie.

Me: NO!

Mummy: It's just that we've been here nearly three hours now . . .

Me: NO!

Mummy: We have to go home at some point, Archie.

Me: WTF is your problem?!

Mummy: We can't live at the park, Archie!

Me: I live at park!

Mummy: You'd be a bit cold sleeping here, darling.

Me: I sleep at park!

Mummy: Come on now, we need to get home for dinner.

Me: I HATE DINNER!

Mummy: Other people might like to have a go on the swings, you know . . .

Me: I HATE PEOPLE!

Mummy: Archie, I said it's time to go home now. Come on!

Me: *throws self onto the ground, deactivates limbs and goes absolutely apeshit*

Mummy: *picks me up and tries to get me into the buggy, fails, proceeds to carry me home under one arm, pushing the buggy and balancing the scooter over her shoulder while I claw the skin off her face with my little razor-like nails*

Same thing happens every time but she never learns . . . Next time, take a tent!

SATURDAY, 13 MAY

Mummy said that now I'm two and a half and I'm going to be a big brother I get to do big-boy things! One of those things is saying 'bye-bye to nappies!' so we are going on a shopping trip today so I can pick my own 'special big-boy pants'.

Why is my life so degrading?

SUNDAY, 14 MAY

First day of wearing my new digger pants. Changed my mind and decided I wanted the football pants that we didn't end up getting. Refused to put them on until Daddy went to town and swapped them.

Mummy surprised me with a potty that looks like a turtle and sings songs and claps every time you do a wee or poo on it. How old do they think I am – two?!

I managed one wee on it but then the song started making me ragey so I pissed on the sofa.

Then I pissed on the carpet.

Then I pissed in my toy box.

Then I emptied my bowels in the middle of Sunday lunch. So funny!

Mummy seemed upset that I didn't seem to rate the singing potty. I mean . . . would she like it if the toilet clapped every time she did a shit?! I think not.

MONDAY, 15 MAY

Got through eight changes of clothes by lunchtime
- go me!

Just going to keep on pissing in my pants until
they stop with this ludicrous notion that I should
be responsible for my own bladder. Heard Mummy say
to Daddy that it should get better in a few days
and they have to hold firm because going back to
nappies would mean starting all over again.

Have also decided to start biting again.

TUESDAY, 16 MAY

Woke up at 4.35 a.m.

Bit Ella for blocking the slide.

Pissed on Daddy's Xbox One.

WEDNESDAY, 17 MAY

Woke up at 4.37 a.m.

Bit Ben for taking the last bit of banana.

Pissed in Mummy's favourite shoes.

THURSDAY, 18 MAY

Woke up at 4.04 a.m.

Bit Harry because of his stupid face.

Did a poo right next to the potty.

FRIDAY, 19 MAY

2.19 a.m. Had a terrible nightmare about the singing potty. It tore through the house on a violent rampage!

I couldn't sleep again after that. Watched *Fireman Sam* until the sun came up. It was beautiful.

7 a.m. Back in nappies. No longer biting. Life is good.

Apparently they'll try again later on when I'm a little bit older as it'll be easier then.

Hmmm.

SATURDAY, 20 MAY

Still feeling slightly traumatised by the axe-wielding potty. Mummy put it in the cupboard underneath the stairs to try and alleviate my fears.

9.17 p.m. Can't sleep! Keep worrying it might get out in the night and try and kill us all!

11.43 p.m. Daddy took it out of the cupboard, bashed it on the head with a hammer and said, 'WELL IT'S DEAD NOW!' in a really angry voice. Now I'm scared of Daddy so I had to sleep in bed with Mummy.

He will have to sleep on the sofa until I can trust him again.

SUNDAY, 21 MAY

Agreed to sleep in my own bed only if Mummy sat
with me until I was asleep. It ended up being a
really fun game actually.

First we spent about forty-five minutes talking
about all sorts of interesting things like 'Why do
people poo?' and 'Why is poo brown?' and 'Can you
eat poo?' etc. etc. Then we did some singing and
some 'I spy', which was actually quite hard as it
was so dark, and then Mummy did this fake cross
voice that kept going 'I'm not kidding, Archie,
I'm going to get really angry soon!' while I did
some hysterical laughter.

Then I'd go silent for a bit and slow my breathing
down until it was almost like I was asleep but it
was all just a sneaky trick because I was actually
pretending!!

Then Mummy would do this really funny commando
crawl to the door like she was a soldier in the
army and then just as she opened the door to try
and squeeze herself out I'd pop up out of bed and

go 'NEVER EVER LEAVE ME!!!!!!!!!!' and then we'd
start the whole thing again from the beginning.

Absolutely hilarious. Looking forward to playing
again tomorrow.

WEDNESDAY, 24 MAY

Been playing 'Mummy and Archie's Bedtime Game' all week. Loving it! Daddy was obviously jealous and wanted to get involved too but it's a special bonding time for me and Mummy so I just went ballistic until he fucked off.

THURSDAY, 25 MAY

Very funny, Mummy. Very. Funny.

FRIDAY, 26 MAY

I am going to Granny's for a sleepover tomorrow!
No special reason – just apparently Mummy is a bit
tired.

SATURDAY, 27 MAY

Mummy gave Granny a list of my routines and a bunch of meals to defrost and told Granny that I must eat all of my dinner before I have any treats and that I shouldn't have much sugar because sugar makes me go crazy like a honey badger (which is incidentally my spirit animal).

I don't know why she even bothers. We all know Granny just puts it all straight in the bin.

Anyway, what a lovely time me and Granny had!

Granny even let me take the iPad to bed and I fell asleep watching Thomas the Tank Engine unboxing videos on YouTube. Bliss!

SUNDAY, 28 MAY

Ate chocolate spread on toast for breakfast and then Granny let me eat some right out of the jar. I wish I could live at Granny's: it is so much more relaxed at her house.

Mummy came to pick me up just as I was finishing off a large bag of Tangfastics for my lunch – she didn't look very pleased and did a face where she pursed her lips together like a cat's bum-hole.

Granny said, 'It's a grandmother's right to spoil her grandson and if you don't like it then perhaps you shouldn't leave Archie here in the first place!' Touché – I love Granny, she's so badass!

8.45 p.m. Still awake. I feel wired!!

10.01 p.m. Starving hungry. Shout down for more Tangfastics. No response apart from muffled sobbing.

MONDAY, 29 MAY

Another bank holiday. Daddy muttered something about the 'beforetime' and having a nice lie-in and then going out for 'brunch', which is like breakfast for lazy people, and then getting pissed all afternoon. He laughed and then looked a bit sad like he was going to cry.

To cheer him up I suggested we spend the next four hours playing tea parties. He seemed really happy after that.

WEDNESDAY, 31 MAY

Mummy looks absolutely dreadful.

Daddy said that growing the baby is hard work, which is why Mummy has been feeling quite tired and sick lately. I just assumed she'd been a bit heavy with the gin to be honest.

I am meant to be nice and considerate to her for the next few months as she is doing a very important job. I'm always nice and considerate towards Mummy so I'm not quite sure what he means?!

FRIDAY, 2 JUNE

Lucy came round today for a cup of tea and to talk about baby plans. She is really enjoying being pregnant and is feeling fantastic!

It will be Lucy's first baby, which is lovely, especially as she already knows everything there is to know about being a perfect parent.

My mummy is doing a pretty decent job to be fair, but it's always good to keep them on their toes and remind them who is boss. I see a few of the kids at nursery blindly following orders and it makes me really sad. I mean, how will your parents ever properly respect you if you voluntarily eat spinach?!

SATURDAY, 3 JUNE

Today when I woke up Mummy said she had a surprise for me and it turned out that we are going to Peppa Pig World. I could hardly breathe I was that excited. My only problem was that we were not immediately there.

Unfortunately Mummy had failed to invent a teleportation system for the trip so we had to take the goddamn car. I was relatively cross but passed the time singing the 'Bing Bong Song' repeatedly and asking for updates of how long it would take.

When we arrived at the theme park I was immediately struck by its beauty – it looked like a rainbow had puked up over everything. But things started to go downhill from there – the rides looked immense but you had to queue up for them. My time is incredibly scarce and I do not wish to spend it standing in a line! Kids everywhere were going crazy – there were punch-ups, pinching and a lot of verbal abuse. Mummy said it reminded her of queuing up to get into Illusions nightclub on a Saturday night circa 1999.

George's Dinosaur Adventure was boss but we had
to spend fifteen minutes waiting for Grandpa Pig's
Boat Trip – what a pile of wank.

Later on in the day Mummy asked if I'd like to
meet Peppa. I excitedly elbowed three people
in the face to get to her, only to find myself
extremely disappointed – she just bumbled around
like a gormless buffoon.

They tried to make me have a photo taken with her
but due to her astounding arrogance I refused.
I was so cross and sad that I became hysterical
and then did a rage vomit all over her feet (I'd

also had about three Fruit Shoots and a bag of candy floss by this point, which may or may not be relevant).

Next Daddy took me to the toilets to clean me up and someone turned on a hand-dryer next to my face. I think you can predict the rest.

Then it was time to leave. Mummy had to spend £87 in the gift shop as means of compensation for the psychological trauma suffered.

They say never meet your heroes for a reason!

SUNDAY, 4 JUNE

3.37 a.m. Had another nightmare – this time about the ill-fated Peppa Pig World visit.

The huge mute Peppa and her team of crazy hand-dryers were chasing me and taunting me. Was horrific.

TUESDAY, 6 JUNE

Brilliant day. Was walking down the street and saw a dog taking a shit. Watched it come right out – epic.

Much better than Peppa Pig World and you didn't have to pay!

FRIDAY, 9 JUNE

As I've got older I've noticed that my repertoire of favourite foods has decreased. I guess it's just a case of my taste buds maturing and recognising the finer foods of the world. I am also becoming much more aware of the sneaky tricks Mummy does to get me to eat foods I do not like (such as blitzing vegetables into meals and calling them stupid names like 'X-Ray-Vision Carrots' or 'Tasty Treetops' or 'Mr Parsnip Pants' – what even . . .?!)

Anyway, I have therefore decided to toughen up my personal food consumption policies.

To whom it may concern:

I shall not be eating anything except the following until further notice:

1. Coco Pops

2. Pesto pasta

3. Chicken nuggets

4. Biscuits (any)

5. Quavers

6. Tangfastics

7. Ice-cream (no bits)

Seems to cover all the basic food groups to me. I'm pretty sure a handful of Tangfastics fulfils your five a day.

SATURDAY, 10 JUNE

Stuck to my new diet rigidly all day. Quite surprised at my willpower! Mummy seems slightly frustrated by it, though.

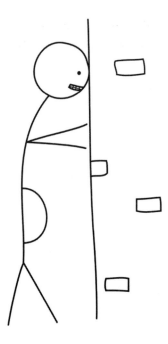

SUNDAY, 11 JUNE

Granny came for Sunday lunch – it was chicken, potato, broccoli and carrots. Looked absolutely gross so I refused to eat it.

Granny said, 'In my day you got fed what you were given and if you didn't like it then you went hungry!'

Not quite sure what she's on about as we both know full well that I live off biscuits and cakes at her house. But hey ho.

Mummy says she's going to play hardball from now on.

MONDAY, 12 JUNE

Didn't eat anything at all today except half a banana and four raisins – suck on that, Annabel Karmel!

TUESDAY, 13 JUNE

Woke up starving but determined to stick to my guns. Mummy idiotically served up porridge for breakfast – that went down well.

Then they packed me off to nursery. My eyes started to roll back in my head, so weak was I that I could no longer stand; I lay on the floor moaning . . .

Thank goodness for Jasmine, someone who is actually concerned with my wellbeing.

They called Mummy at work and asked her to come and pick me up. Next time I'll ask them to call 999 and she can explain to the staff at A&E why she is trying to starve me to death – that'll learn her.

Anyway, it worked. I got pesto pasta and two bags of Quavers for lunch.

Archie: 1

Mummy: 0

THURSDAY, 15 JUNE

Mummy was looking a bit deflated today so I went up to her and told her she had nice-smelling knees. Seemed to cheer her up a bit – she's so needy and pathetic.

FRIDAY, 16 JUNE

The more *Postman Pat* I watch, the more irritated I become with the absolute cretin! It's finally reached a point where I can't stay silent any longer, so I've drafted him a strongly worded letter of complaint!

Dear Pat,

I have tried to contact you via Royal Mail but they are under the illusion that Greendale is a fictional place – what's up with that?! You may find this letter a tad harsh but I feel I need to write to address you directly as your friends, family and colleagues seem unwilling or unable to give you any constructive feedback.

Let's cut to the chase. You are crap at your job and I have absolutely no idea how you managed to blag your promotion to Head of Special Delivery Services. You consistently lose, damage and/or open parcels you have been entrusted to deliver, which is both stupid and illegal. Before you protest I have listed a few examples of your incompetence that have particularly riled me:

1. *You severely delayed the start of Amy's Animal Day after you opened your van to check that the fruit bats you were delivering were OK. Quelle surprise, they flew away, and you dicked about for god knows how long trying to tempt them back into the van with apples. Poor Amy was beside herself; it was the highlight of her year!*

2. *You failed to secure the doors of your van and lost Michael's film for his open-air movie night. You thought that showing a movie of yourself entitled* Postman Pat – Movie Star, *made by some kids, was a suitable alternative. It was actually extremely arrogant AND you didn't even say sorry.*

3. *Lizzie was incredibly nervous about her music recital and was depending on you to deliver her piano on time so she could practise. You were very late and she fudged it up but yet again you were hailed hero of the day.*

4. *You delivered a single pair of ice-skates to that spoilt bitch Meera by, er, HELICOPTER*

*(!!!). How can this possibly be cost
effective? Was this actually sanctioned by
Royal Mail?*

5. *On the day of the re-opening of Pencaster
Town Hall you were tasked with making two (!)
deliveries at the same time. Before the episode
even panned out we all knew this was way beyond
your scope. After successfully delivering some
oil to Ted (well done) you were desperate to
show him the balloons for the celebration
in the back of your van . . . Oh dear, they
floated out. PC Selby then became entangled in
them and drifted off into the sky; you seemed
pleased, as rescuing him was an excuse to use
the helicopter again! It was just another
ridiculous sequence of events that could only
have happened to you, and somehow you came
out of it better than if you had just made the
straightforward delivery?!?!?!??!!?*

*These are just a few examples; there are many
more, believe me. I am left flabbergasted at the
end of each episode when, instead of issuing
demands for compensation, everyone cheers you on
while you arrogantly smirk 'Special Delivery –
mission accomplished!' Yeh, BY THE SKIN OF YOUR
FRICKING TEETH!*

What really takes the biscuit is that rather than giving you a disciplinary or a performance review, Ben decides to throw you a special party and presents you with the prestigious award of a Special Delivery Services Gold Star. He says, and I quote, 'Pat's the best of the best, he's never been late with a delivery!'

Are they seeing what I'm seeing?!?!? What kind of hold do you have over these people?!

OK, OK, I watch a little too much of your new SDS show, but I'm two – what the hell else is there to do? That's what worries me the most – you are a role model to pre-schoolers whose biggest dream is to become an incompetent postman with access to a quad bike and a snowmobile – it's nothing short of delusional.

In light of the above I'd like to suggest you offer your resignation. Mrs Goggins, I'm sure, would be a suitable replacement.

Yours sincerely,

Archie Adams

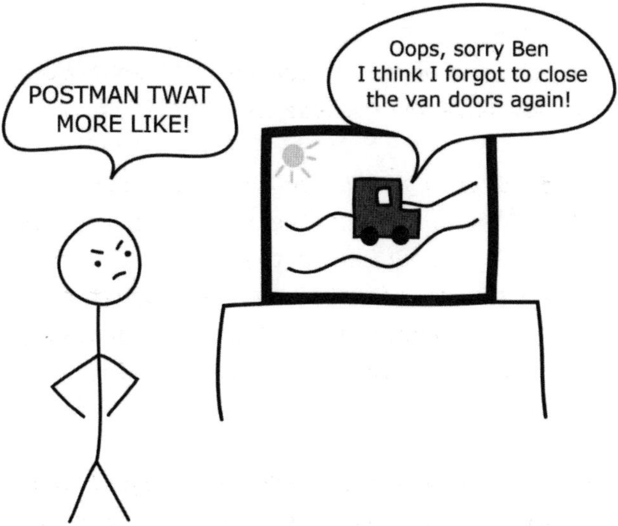

POSTMAN TWAT MORE LIKE!
Oops, sorry Ben I think I forgot to close the van doors again!

SUNDAY, 18 JUNE - FATHER'S DAY

Today is the day that we celebrate Daddy. Not quite sure why, seeing as he is never fucking here. He just waltzes off every morning waxing lyrical about 'meetings' and 'conference calls' and then waltzes back in at teatime talking about how important he is and how nothing can get done properly without him.

Even Mummy doesn't seem to have a fucking clue what his job actually involves, but apparently it's necessary he's there because of something to do with money, bills, needing food to eat and boring stuff like that.

We made cards at nursery last week but I couldn't be bothered to do mine so I just brought all the bits home in an envelope for him to make it himself. I still think he seems pretty pointless and TBH Mummy is my favourite.

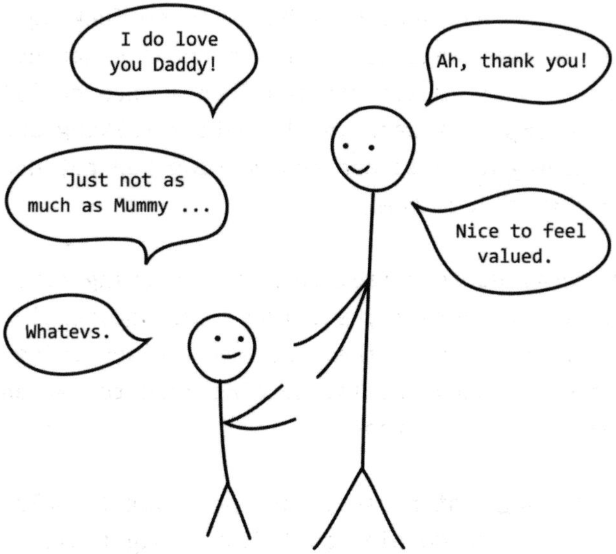
I do love you Daddy!
Ah, thank you!
Just not as much as Mummy ...
Nice to feel valued.
Whatevs.

WEDNESDAY, 21 JUNE

Got up at 4.11 a.m. to mark the summer solstice. It's been getting so bright in the mornings – lovin' it!

Due to the early start we had eaten our lunch by 10.25 a.m. which I think is a new record.

THURSDAY, 22 JUNE

Mummy ordered me a pair of Crocs on the internet and they arrived today. I opened them excitedly only to be hugely disappointed.

When I made my displeasure clear Mummy said, 'You specifically chose yellow ones, Archie!'

I did. Yes I did – but they were just not what I expected. Something about the shade or the texture just didn't feel at all right. The longer I looked at them the angrier I got.

'You won't be getting any others so you'd better wear them, Archie!' she said.

I will not wear them! They are offensive to my very being. I HATE THEM. THEY ARE ALL WRONG. I SHALL **NEVER** WEAR THEM!

FRIDAY, 23 JUNE

SATURDAY, 24 JUNE

SUNDAY, 25 JUNE

MONDAY, 26 JUNE

I LOVE THEM, I LOVE THEM, I LOVE THEM! THANK YOU
SO MUCH, MUMMY!

I shall wear them all the time including in the
bath, in my bed, and in all sorts of inappropriate
weather conditions.

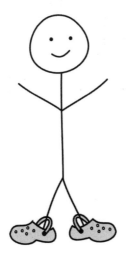

WEDNESDAY, 28 JUNE

Still no reply from Pat. Will try the Citizens Advice Bureau.

THURSDAY, 29 JUNE

We are going on a holiday tomorrow. Apparently I've only just been told because I'm not very good at being patient.

Daddy said, 'It's a nice chance for us all to relax,' which made Mummy snort.

A thing called 'packing' happens, which seemed to make everyone hate each other and random inanimate objects such as shoes and charging devices.

FRIDAY, 30 JUNE

We set off to our destination in the south of France - apparently the drive was going to take a 'VERY long time' so I kept tabs on our progress by repeatedly asking for updates.

After we had been in the car for a while I started feeling unwell and sicked up loads of big lumps of semi-digested breakfast. We couldn't stop due to the motorway so we had to drive for ages with lots of crying and everyone feeling sick due to the disgusting sick smell.

When we finally found somewhere to stop, Mummy started changing my clothes and Daddy wandered off. She said, 'You have got to be kidding me!' He came back later with a coffee the size of his head, which Mummy said was 'bloody ridiculous'. I wonder if when I grow up, I will get angry about the size of drinks other people buy too.

Then we drove our car onto a boat and the boat went over the sea – absolutely mad!!!

Afterwards we did a bit more driving before spending the night in a motel, which is like a cheapo hotel on the edge of a motorway. It was supposed to be so Daddy could get some rest after a long drive but it was such a rare treat to sleep in one room together that we all ended up talking in the dark for hours!

Having a fabulous time so far!

SATURDAY, 1 JULY

After some more driving we arrived at our 'gîte', which sounds posh but it is basically like some sort of stone shed with furniture in it. It has sketchy Wi-Fi which is also 'bloody ridiculous' and causes Mummy to have a tech tantrum similar to when I throw the iPad on the floor in a rage when it runs out of battery, or when Daddy kicks the Xbox because he loses on FIFA.

Some strange things I've learned about France so far: they drive on the wrong side of the road and eat cross ants for breakfast. Very odd.

SUNDAY, 2 JULY

We spend most of the day either in the swimming pool or talking about when we are going to go swimming again.

I've noticed so far that a holiday seems to be about getting more shouty than usual and Daddy drinking beer all day. Apparently because the bottles over here are smaller than the ones in England 'they hardly even count!'

Mummy says in retrospect France was a really depressing place to come while pregnant because she can't have all of her favourite things like cheese, cured meats and wine. I can't have all my favourite things either like CBeebies, Netflix and Quavers, but you don't see me complaining (much).

MONDAY, 3 JULY

At home we have a thing called 'triple protection' on my bedroom windows, which is blackout curtains, a blackout blind and blackout material gaffer-taped right onto the panes. Here the curtains are pretty thin, which is great as it makes the days longer, meaning more time for having fun!

Mummy said, 'The swimming pool doesn't open at 5 a.m. and asking every five minutes is not going to change that!' While we waited for swimming, Mummy drank lots of 'pointless' decaffeinated coffee and looked like she was going to cry. God love her.

Later on we took a picnic to the beach. We were all having great fun building sandcastles until I dropped my banana in the sand.

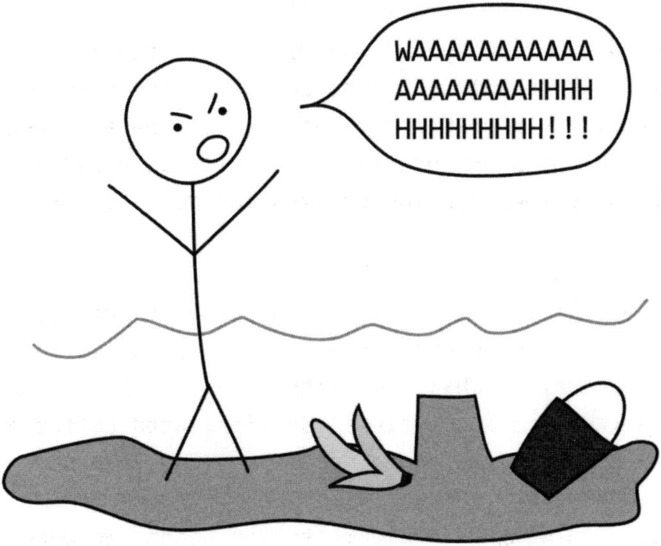
WAAAAAAAAAAAA
AAAAAAAAAHHHH
HHHHHHHHH!!!

TUESDAY, 4 JULY

It was raining so we went to an aquarium to look at fish. I didn't like it because fish don't even do anything at all so I just lay down on the floor and refused to move until we left.

For lunch we went out for crepes, which I wouldn't eat even though it's 'all the exact same things I have at home'. I don't care – they looked strange. For the rest of the holiday I am going to refuse to eat anything except chicken nuggets and ice-cream, because I am suspicious of France and its strange ways.

In the afternoon we played a really good game of hide 'n' seek. I ran off into the crowd at a busy French market and hid under a table for forty-five minutes. Took them ages to find me, they were getting themselves into a right panic. Eventually they ended up calling the Police Nationale! It was quite funny actually as Mummy and Daddy were the ones that got told off and I got to sit inside their car and put the sirens on – result!

WEDNESDAY, 5 JULY

Spent four hours in the pool playing 'crazy shark chase game'. A good day.

THURSDAY, 6 JULY

We went on a day trip to see some poxy ruins. Everyone looked bored. Apparently it's just so we can say we did something cultural. We should have just gone swimming, they all know it too.

FRIDAY, 7 JULY

We go swimming in the morning and in the
afternoon and eat chicken nuggets and ice-cream
as it's 'just not worth the battle any
more'. #Winning

SATURDAY, 8 JULY

Packing happened again. There was a lot of muttering. Daddy is a '[something something] idiot!' and Mummy should stop being an 'uptight witch!'

About 10 minutes into the journey we drove past a McDonald's and Mummy said it was probably the first time she has been on holiday and not had a Big Mac. She seemed pleased, in a way. Apparently it's fun going in and seeing all the different things they have on their menu but I don't really understand why anyone eats anything other than chicken nuggets anyway.

Then I made them stop for chicken nuggets.

I passed the rest of the time in the car by kicking Daddy in the back of his seat and asking for my DVDs to be swapped over every five minutes. It made him go all cross and confused and we ended up taking a 'scenic detour through the Alps'. Mummy said it wasn't a scenic detour and that what had actually happened was that we were very fucking lost. Then she had to get out of the car for a good old yodelling session which Daddy said made her sound a bit like Heidi: the unhinged version.

SUNDAY, 9 JULY

We are back home and have reliable Wi-Fi so everyone is visibly happier.

MONDAY, 10 JULY

As I write this, Mummy is having an actual argument with the laundry basket. Very disturbing.

TUESDAY, 11 JULY

I've come to the conclusion that most parents seem to think of their children as performing monkeys. It's always 'Show Auntie Viv your walking!', 'Show Granny your wave!', 'Show this random lady in the supermarket a little piece of your soul!'

They use their children as pawns in some sort of pointless game where there are no winners. I do not give a rat's arse if eighteen-month-old Emilia know how to recite the alphabet backwards in three different languages – she just sounds dull as fuck to me.

I refuse to take part in their petty competitions.

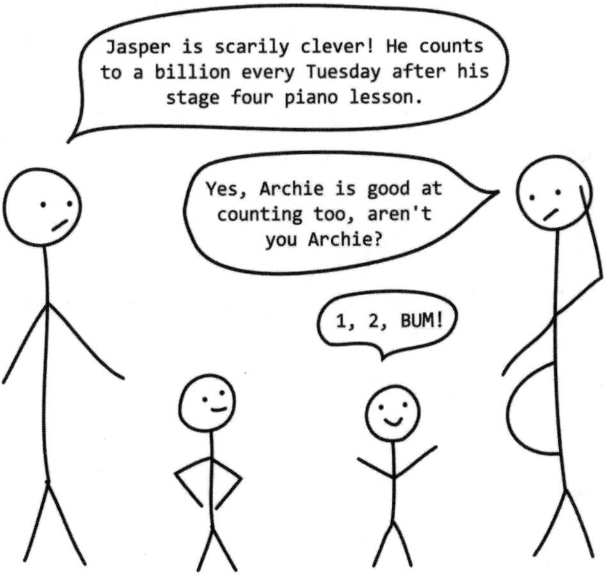
Jasper is scarily clever! He counts to a billion every Tuesday after his stage four piano lesson.
Yes, Archie is good at counting too, aren't you Archie?
1, 2, BUM!

WEDNESDAY, 12 JULY

Went out into the garden and stamped on a bunch of woodlice. Really enjoyed it. What is wrong with me?

THURSDAY, 13 JULY

Told Amelie about my woodlouse killing spree. She thought it might be indicative of cereal killer tendencies.

Not sure what she means but it sounds kind of fun?

MONDAY, 17 JULY

I have been worrying about this whole getting pregnant thing again. I mean what if I end up with a baby in my tummy?! Yuk.

I decided to press Mummy for some more answers and found out that apparently Daddy has some seeds and he gives them to her to mix with one of her eggs and that makes a baby.

All totally clear then! Not.

I asked her where he gets the seeds from and how she mixes them with her egg and she went all weird and said perhaps it's best to have a man-to-man chat with Daddy.

Later on when Daddy got home I asked him where he gets his seeds from and he laughed and said he keeps them in his magic sack!

WTAF?!?!

FRIDAY, 21 JULY

This morning Mummy and Daddy casually dropped into conversation that they were going out with friends for dinner. Apparently the babysitter was coming round at 8 p.m. and they'd be back before I even noticed. Then they put on some sort of weird, forlorn/hard-done-by expressions and said that they were really looking forward to it as they haven't been out together for ages.

What did they want me to do – get a tiny violin out?!?

You have kids, you pay the price . . . and that means no more social life. Ever.

Here's something I've learned: if you try really, really hard you can channel all of your inner strength into spiking a fever on demand.

I know. Such bad luck.
It's nearly 39 degrees poor thing.
Yeh ... another time maybe.
Woe is me!

WEDNESDAY, 26 JULY

It was parents' evening tonight at nursery. I think it went really well.

First Jasmine showed them some of my best pieces of artwork from the year:

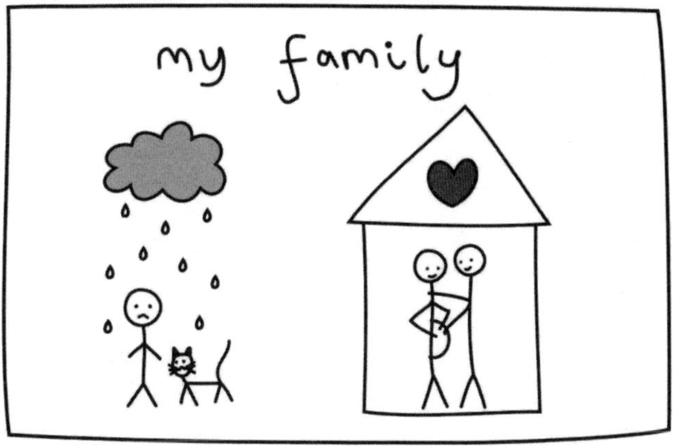
my family

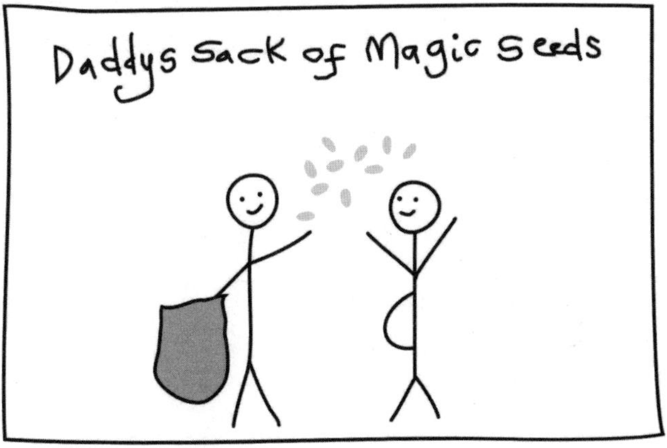
Daddys sack of Magic seeds

Then we talked about my future career aspirations.

SATURDAY, 29 JULY

Dinner was an absolute farce again tonight. Apparently I am making everyone 'sick to the back teeth' with my 'ridiculous mealtime antics!' yet they continue to make the same mistakes AGAIN and AGAIN.

I am getting so fed up with their inability to accommodate my needs that I have drafted them a letter listing my humble requirements:

To whom it may concern:

- My plate – I hate it. I don't care what colour you choose, it's always wrong. Scrape the food off, put that one in the dishwasher and bring me the one I ask for. OK, now I've changed my mind, I want the original one back out of the dishwasher; clean it first, please. Actually I think I'd prefer a bowl.

- Why have you given me a toddler fork? I don't eat with baby cutlery any more – I'm nearly three now, you twat. I'll have a proper fork. In fact I'll take two as I like to rotate.

- I know I don't NEED a knife but I like stabbing
  things so I'll take three of those. Then when
  I stab my own self in the hand please accept
  responsibility immediately. I mean why would you
  give your two-year-old a knife? You're an idiot
  and I'm calling the police.

- I don't like my cup – I want the Winnie the Pooh
  one you lost at the park in 2015. I hope it's
  not water; I want juice. You know what'll happen
  if you dilute it, right? Actually I don't trust
  you with juice – give me a Fruit Shoot, sealed
  so I know it's not been tampered with. Actually
  are you drinking wine? I'll take your wine.

- Oh hang on, there is stuff on my plate that is
  not beige. This is mealtime 101 – what part of
  it do you not understand?! Get it off.

- Everything is cold now; you took too long
  sorting out my basic requirements. Reheat it.
  Now it's burning my mouth, cool it down. Now
  it's fucking freezing. Reheat it again. Actually
  don't bother – just chuck it in the bin, you've
  messed me around too much and it's just a waste
  of my valuable time.

- Where's my pudding? I don't get pudding?! Sorry
  – WHAT?! If you send me to bed without any food

in my tummy you know I'll just wake up at 3 a.m. asking for Cheerios, right?

- Thank you, a yoghurt and toast will be fine.

- I'm still hungry: give me a packet of Hula Hoops and a KitKat.

Kind regards from a disgruntled diner x

SUNDAY, 30 JULY

They sat me down and explained how babies are made – for real this time. They had taken a book out from the library – it had pictures and everything! It will be a VERY long time before I can look them properly in the face again.

TUESDAY, 1 AUGUST

A weird observation today. I can be totally
content . . .

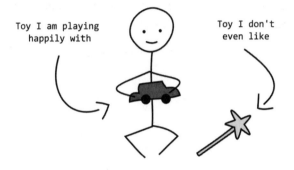

Toy I am playing
happily with

Toy I don't
even like

. . . but when someone else picks up a toy that I previously had zero interest in, it suddenly looks like the best toy that has ever existed in the whole entire world. Strange!

SATURDAY, 5 AUGUST

The doorbell went this morning and it was a massive delivery for Daddy. I have done my best to transcribe the conversation for you below (I have bleeped the ruder words out because to be honest the swearing was quite excessive for my innocent young ears) . . .

Mummy: What the BLEEP is that?!

Daddy: It's a surfboard.

Mummy: What the BLEEP have you bought a surfboard for?!

Daddy: I've decided to take up surfing.

Mummy: *does this sort of fake laughing thing* You have got to be BLEEPING kidding me, right?!

Daddy: *looks a bit scared and pathetic* Errr, no.

Mummy: Have you failed to notice that I am thirty-six weeks pregnant for BLEEPS sake? When the BLEEP

do you think you are going to go BLEEPING surfing?!
Could you not pick a slightly more convenient time
to have a midlife BLEEPING crisis?! Also, we live
in London – there is no BLEEPING sea here, you
BLEEPING imbecile! Are you doing this on purpose
to upset me?! Where the BLEEP are you even going
to keep it?! I can't even begin to . . . I just
can't even . . . just BLEEP off, you inconsiderate
BLEEP!

She didn't even pause for answers, she just
stormed off upstairs and slammed the bedroom door.
Daddy said he'd make her a nice cup of tea and
everything would be fine. Probably.

SUNDAY, 6 AUGUST

Daddy booked Mummy in for a surprise pregnancy massage to help her chill the fuck out a bit. After she'd gone, me and Daddy watched *Point Break* and then we did some grass-surfing in the garden – it was ace!

FRIDAY, 25 AUGUST

It has been a little while since I last wrote. It has been a looooooong hot summer and I have had nothing much to report. Mummy has been on maternity leave, which I thought would mean some quality time together, but apart from the farm trips, the aquarium, soft play, swimming, the park, a host of hideously expensive day trips and a rerun of the infamous Peppa Pig World experience, I have lived virtually like a recluse.

I don't know what's wrong with her - she just seems so . . . lazy!

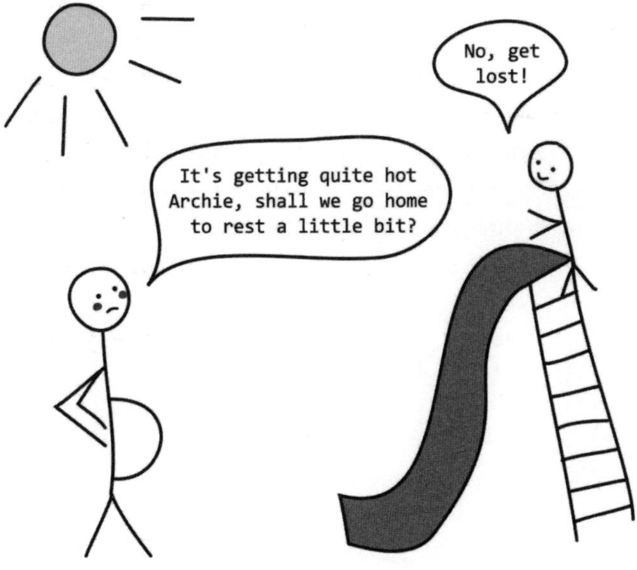
No, get lost!
It's getting quite hot Archie, shall we go home to rest a little bit?

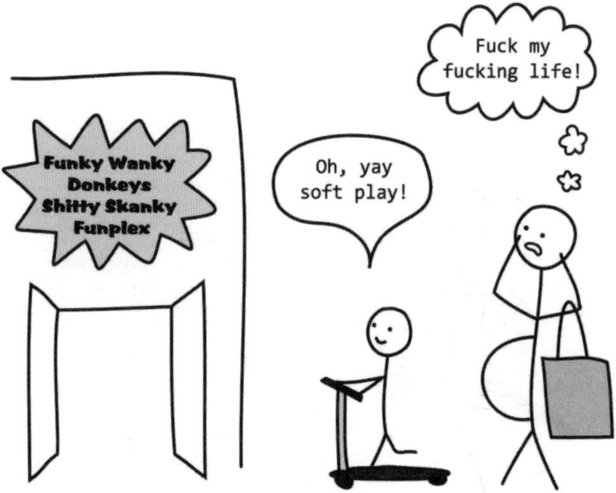
Funky Wanky
Donkeys
Shitty Skanky
Funplex
Oh, yay
soft play!
Fuck my
fucking life!

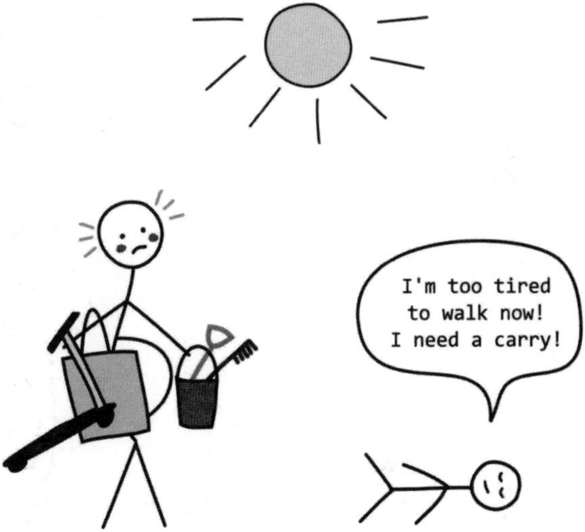
I'm too tired
to walk now!
I need a carry!

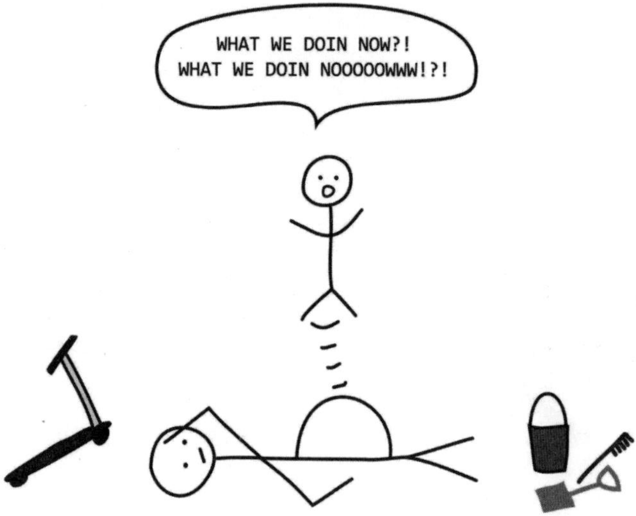
WHAT WE DOIN NOW?!
WHAT WE DOIN NOOOOOWWW!?!

SATURDAY, 26 AUGUST

In other news, the parasite grows bigger by the day. I can see its limbs slide across Mummy's abdomen from inside like something out of a horror film. They ask me to touch Mummy's tummy to feel the baby move, but it repulses me.

SUNDAY, 27 AUGUST

3.31 a.m. BAD DREAMS!!!!

MONDAY, 28 AUGUST

'Why do I bother?'
A haiku by Archie Adams, aged 2¾

Wind blows through the trees.
The iPad has not been charged.
My day is ruined.

THURSDAY, 31 AUGUST

More of the same.

Mummy looks round like a ball and can hardly even move. Her legs are like sausages and she groans whenever she tries to get up off the sofa.

She is practically living off sardine, tomato ketchup and gherkin sandwiches, which smell so disgusting I don't even know where to begin.

Daddy is constantly getting it in the neck. Mummy calls him an idiot a lot, and worse things like 'can't' with a 'u' where the 'a' is. I'm not sure what it means but apparently it's 'fucking out of order and you can't go around being a total bitch all of the goddamn time just because you're pregnant!'

SATURDAY, 2 SEPTEMBER

I think Mummy has well and truly lost the plot.
Caught her worshipping a bottle of gin today.
Utterly barmy, I tell you.

SUNDAY, 3 SEPTEMBER

Daddy made us all a lovely lunch and Mummy ended up having a go at us both because I was dropping crumbs everywhere and he was chewing in a really annoying way. We can't seem to do anything right! Perhaps me and Daddy have more in common than I thought.

He told me that Mummy has lots of hormones flying around her system and they make her turn into a bit of a nut job. Mummy heard him . . . I don't think it's necessary to go into details about the events that transpired, but to put it mildly it wasn't her finest hour.

TUESDAY, 5 SEPTEMBER

Asked Jasmine at nursery what 'can't' with a 'u' instead of an 'a' means and she said it means that she might need to get Mummy and Daddy in for a little chat.

WEDNESDAY, 6 SEPTEMBER

Mummy's birthday today. She didn't look too happy. Maybe it's because she's thirty-six and that's pretty much halfway dead.

I wracked my brains to think of something to do to cheer her up. Then I had the perfect idea!

It was a bit off the wall but I think she liked it.

THURSDAY, 7 SEPTEMBER

We were talking about evolution today at nursery.
Apparently we all changed into humans from monkeys
and it struck me that it's sort of like what is
happening to Mummy, except in reverse.

Is she devolving back into an ape?

The devolution of the pregnant primate

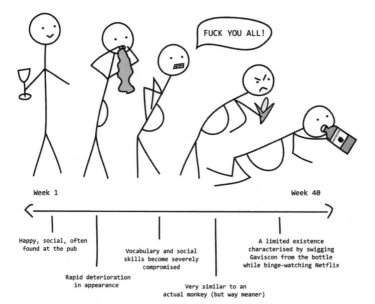

Week 1

FUCK YOU ALL!

Week 40

Happy, social, often
found at the pub

Rapid deterioration
in appearance

Vocabulary and social
skills become severely
compromised

Very similar to an
actual monkey (but way meaner)

A limited existence
characterised by swigging
Gaviscon from the bottle
while binge-watching Netflix

FRIDAY, 8 SEPTEMBER

Lucy has had her baby. There was no need for drugs, as apparently it just practically fell out of her vagina.

We went round to meet it today and although it is only three days old it already sleeps through the night, has four-hourly feeds and never really cries.

Shame it's really fucking ugly.

She has also had her placenta made into muffins to give to visitors so they can feel connected to the baby forever. How lovely.

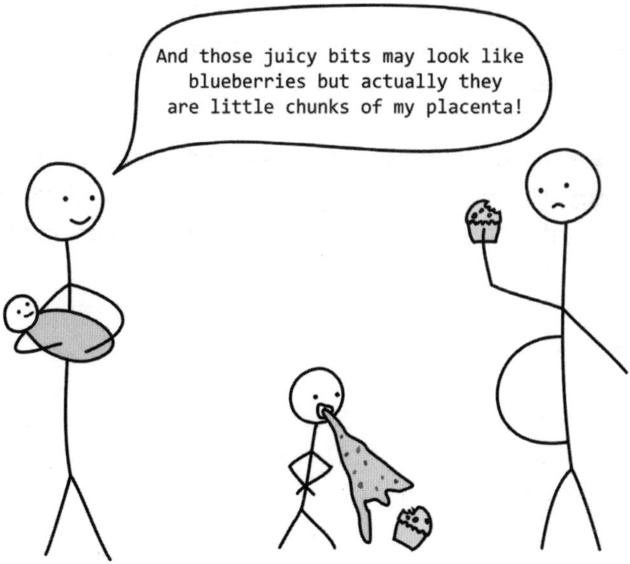
And those juicy bits may look like blueberries but actually they are little chunks of my placenta!

SUNDAY, 10 SEPTEMBER

Apparently 'it' could arrive at any time now. I feel quite forlorn that the days of it being just me and Mummy are drawing to a close . . . so I am following her EVERYWHERE 24/7 - no cheeky nap on the sofa left undisturbed, no toilet door left unopened.

FYI, if 'it' turns out to be a girl then I am leaving. Still holding on to a small sliver of hope that it might be a dog.

MONDAY, 11 SEPTEMBER

Mummy said Daddy should 'have a go at being pregnant if you think you'd be so great at it!'

Daddy would 'hopefully be a bit more bloody upbeat about it than you!'

Then he got a colander thrown at his head.

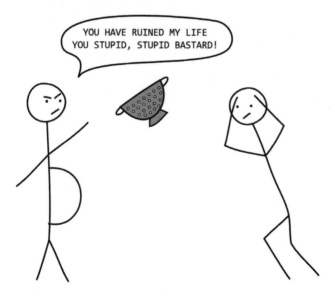

TUESDAY, 12 SEPTEMBER

Amelie says my sibling gender preferences are rude and prove I am not a 'femimist', which is really shameful in this day and age.

I asked her what a femimist is and she said she wasn't really sure but it's the reason why her mummy won't let her play with Barbies that look like sex workers. Apparently playing with unicorns is fine because unicorns are usually very progressive in their views.

WEDNESDAY, 13 SEPTEMBER

Bloody hell – come on, baby! If you don't come soon I think we are going to have to hold a controlled explosion!

STAND BACK SHE'S GONNA BLOW!!!!

THURSDAY, 14 SEPTEMBER

Woke up this morning and found Granny in the house and Mummy and Daddy gone! She said they had a surprise for me and took me to the hospital to meet the new (human ☹) baby. World's shittest surprise seeing as it's all they've been banging on about for months.

The double blow was that it turned out to be a girl. Was not impressed in the slightest but tried to contain my disappointment for fear of being accused of not being a femimist again.

Asked if the baby is still going to be called Chase and they laughed – RUDE!

Apparently she's going to be called Olivia, which is a rubbish name. Going to call her Chase anyway.

The only good thing about today was that the baby bought me the Paw Patroller Deluxe Lorry. I find it slightly hard to believe that a small, useless, immobile thing went down to Toys R Us two hours after being born, but who am I to look a gift horse in the mouth?

FRIDAY, 15 SEPTEMBER

Mummy and Chase came home from hospital. Daddy says he is having two weeks off to spend with us at home – why?!

Verdict on Chase thus far – incredibly pointless. Just does absolutely nothing.

Mummy on the other hand can't walk properly and looks like she's been in a car crash. Poor cow.

SATURDAY, 16 SEPTEMBER

Chase is eating her. She's biting her and making her cry out in pain! Must be some sort of spawn of the devil?!

Apparently it's nothing to worry about and she's just feeding her milk – sucking the life out of her more like!

Why does no one stop this abomination?

SUNDAY, 17 SEPTEMBER

Granny, Auntie Mandy, Uncle Dave and the cousins came round to visit. They all seemed to love the baby. I don't get it! IT STILL DOESN'T DO ANYTHING!

If it was in the wild it would have been eaten by a lion by now - that is how utterly useless it is.

I can do stuff, why doesn't anyone want to look at me?!

MONDAY, 18 SEPTEMBER

Today Mummy started prodding her lovely snuggly belly and said it looked like a deflated balloon. I'd not even noticed TBH but if you've just grown a whole human in there what do you expect?! Give yourself a break, woman!

Daddy told her he hadn't thought it was possible to love her any more than he already did – but he did! Then he made up a song for her and insisted I sing it too. I played along because deep down I'm a decent kinda guy . . . however – ewwww! Parents are so nauseating!

TUESDAY, 19 SEPTEMBER

Back to nursery while everyone else sits around at home eating cake and watching telly with Chase, AKA 'my replacement'.

I screamed blue murder as I was dropped off. Oh the abandonment – the pain is real!

(It's not actually real. I just want Mummy to see how selfish she is being.)

WEDNESDAY, 20 SEPTEMBER

A discovery. They are sleeping all together, cocooned in a bubble of love while I rest my weary bones in a cold, dark cell, totally forgotten.

All the important and valued members of the family

Me

FRIDAY, 22 SEPTEMBER

Things you can't do around the baby while it's asleep:

- Talk loudly.

- Scream.

- Scream very loudly.

- Sing songs in a screamy-type voice.

- Perform fighting moves.

- Throw things at it.

- Breathe.

- Exist.

SATURDAY, 23 SEPTEMBER

No one has any time for me any more. They are always feeding the baby, changing the baby, trying to get the baby to sleep. I was playing with the kitchen knives for a good ten minutes today before anyone even noticed.

TUESDAY, 26 SEPTEMBER

Today I did what I refer to as a double guilt whammy. I cried when I got dropped off at nursery and then I cried when I got picked up. This is to make Mummy question whether I am starting to love Jasmine more than I love her.

I really enjoy these types of mind games.

THURSDAY, 28 SEPTEMBER

If there is supposedly 'no room' in the bed for me, then why can't Daddy leave? The fact Mummy favours sharing her bed with a random person she met at Dave's Disco Bar in Costa Blanca to me, HER SON – the one she actually has a genetic connection to – says it all!

SATURDAY, 30 SEPTEMBER

Things you can't do around the baby while it's asleep (cont.):

• Say 'I HATE YOU, BABY' right in its face.

• Tuck its blankets in (in a violent manner).

• Cover its entire face with teddies.

• Stuff bits of ham in its nose and mouth.

• Do ANYTHING which might restrict its airways.

MONDAY, 2 OCTOBER

Daddy's gone back to work. Mummy looks a bit like someone waiting to face a firing squad.

As we've not been spending as much time together since the arrival of Chase, I decided to maximise our special bonding opportunities by giving up my naps.

Mummy does not seem keen.

WEDNESDAY, 4 OCTOBER

Have discovered that if I nap at nursery I have heaps of energy to get through the days when I am at home.

Mummy said she'd prefer it if I did it the other way around.

Well, Mummy, I would prefer it if YOU stopped being so anal about sharing all the time. I mean, why the hell should I give Oscar in the sandpit (who I've never met before) a go with my digger?! And why the hell should I give Lola from playgroup (an acquaintance at best) a bite of my Goodies bar?! I don't see you offering sips of your coffee to complete randoms!

FRIDAY, 6 OCTOBER

Today Mummy and I bumped into Lucy – she was just back from an 8-mile run with her GX4 Super Galactic Sport Off-Roader.

She said she'd been really busy setting up her new business, 'Placenta Puds', and learning to pole dance ... just for fun. Apparently it's really good for your pelvic floor and generalised fitness – not that she really needed to worry as apparently she was back in her size 8 jeans three hours after giving birth. What an inspiration.

I felt it best not to mention that the reason Mummy smelt like a pineapple daiquiri was because she had three days' worth of Batiste Tropical dry shampoo layered on her scalp.

P.S. FWIW, though, Lucy's baby still looks like an Ewok and ours is way cuter (not that I'd ever admit it, of course).

SATURDAY, 7 OCTOBER

Things you can't do around the baby while it's asleep (cont.):

- Feed it Cheesestrings.

- Pour cups of water on it because it looks like it needs a bath.

- Get on the sofa and then try and jump off the sofa and land on the baby.

- Sellotape its eyes shut.

- Drive toy cars over it and say, 'IT'S A ROAD. I LIKE IT BETTER AS A ROAD.'

- Kick it.

SUNDAY, 8 OCTOBER

A tip to share with my fellows today:

If you go to the park and see your mummy or daddy using the trip as an excuse to ignore you and look at their phone, run face first into a swing. Yes it'll hurt, but I promise it'll be worth it when you see the guilt written on their faces because guilt = ice-cream for dinner. It also means they will think twice about not giving you their undivided attention, which to be quite frank, is the very least you deserve. If they prefer scrolling through Instagram to interacting with you then perhaps they shouldn't have had you in the first place. #JustSaying

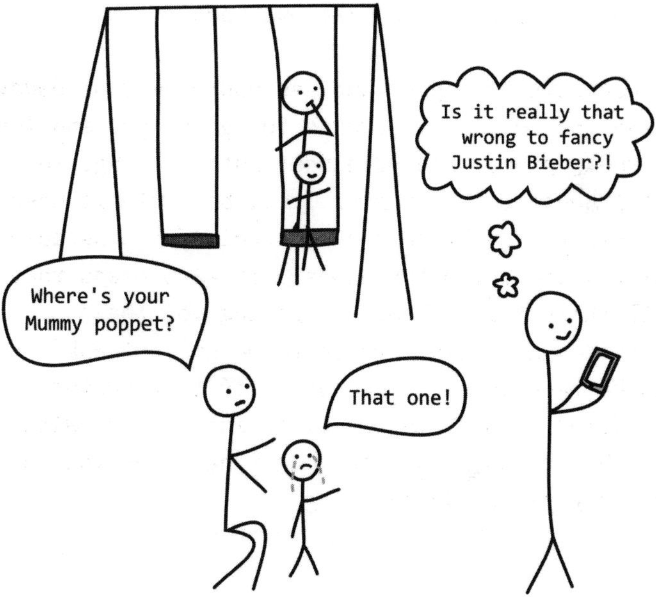
Is it really that wrong to fancy Justin Bieber?!
Where's your Mummy poppet?
That one!

MONDAY, 9 OCTOBER

I was sitting happily watching CBeebies in the living room when I looked down on the floor and what did I see? Yep, Chase on her play mat having the audacity to watch MY TV SHOW. Mummy couldn't understand why I lost the absolute plot. Honestly, I ask you!

THURSDAY, 12 OCTOBER

I don't know if I'm ill or if the baby is sucking life skills out of me but I suddenly feel totally unable to do the most basic of tasks. I can no longer feed myself, I can no longer walk and I can barely string a sentence together – I just keep talking in a really whiny baby voice.

Granny told Mummy it was because I was regressing because I feel left out due to the new baby. Either that or I'm just a total arsehole.

Difficult to tell, really.

FRIDAY, 13 OCTOBER

Daddy said that he and Mummy are feeling very tired because Chase isn't sleeping that well so it'd be really nice if I could try and be a good and helpful boy. Well, that's a bit bloody rich, isn't it?! I guess they've not considered that my sleep is also being affected by that screechy little racket, and guess what? It wasn't my decision to have the baby! You made your bed, you lie in it!!!

SATURDAY, 14 OCTOBER

If you think I'm cross about the new baby you should see Mr Fluffy – he's livid!

Today he did a protest poo in the sink to communicate his displeasure!

SUNDAY, 15 OCTOBER

Following Mr Fluffy's lead I have decided that now might be a good time to totally reverse my potty training.

TUESDAY, 17 OCTOBER

The dirty protests have thus far been ineffective. Amelie reckons when adults don't like each other any more they write 'Dear John' letters to sensitively let each other down and perhaps I should try doing one for the baby as a last-ditch attempt to get rid of it . . .

Dear Chase,

Let's cut to the chase (ha ha! geddit?!) – things were so much better before you got here.

I'm trying to find a kind way to put this but . . . I just hate you. I am therefore terminating your lease and you have thirty days to find alternative accommodation.

All the best for the future!

Your former brother,

Archie

THURSDAY, 19 OCTOBER

There has been no response to the letter. Amelie says another idea is to whack her up on eBay.

One baby, 5 weeks old, bit stinky and loud but otherwise in good working order

Condition: New(ish) with box

£0.99

Enter your max bid

Submit bit

Selling due to contraceptive failure, poor judgment and certain family members not realising how annoying babies could be before having one

Collection only (no returns)

Payments: Credit **Debit** HARIBO

SUNDAY, 22 OCTOBER

Granny came over today for Sunday lunch and a strange thing happened – I said to her that it's funny how chicken is called chicken like the actual animal and she laughed and said it was chicken like the actual animal. Very odd.

She also tried to cuddle the baby a lot. Every time she did it I screamed 'MY GRANNY, GET OFF!' in a really horrible high-pitched voice until she stopped.

TUESDAY, 24 OCTOBER

I told Amelie about the odd chicken thing and she said it was true and that we also eat cows and sheep and pigs too but they are just called different names to distract us from the horror.

She then said that chicken nuggets are the worst as it's all guts and brains and toenails and stuff.

Am devastated – that is pretty much all I eat!

Apparently a guy called Jamie Lolly-Giver stamps on a fairy every time someone eats a chicken nugget.

She also said if I didn't like it I'd have to turn into a vegetable.

Mysteriouser and mysteriouser.

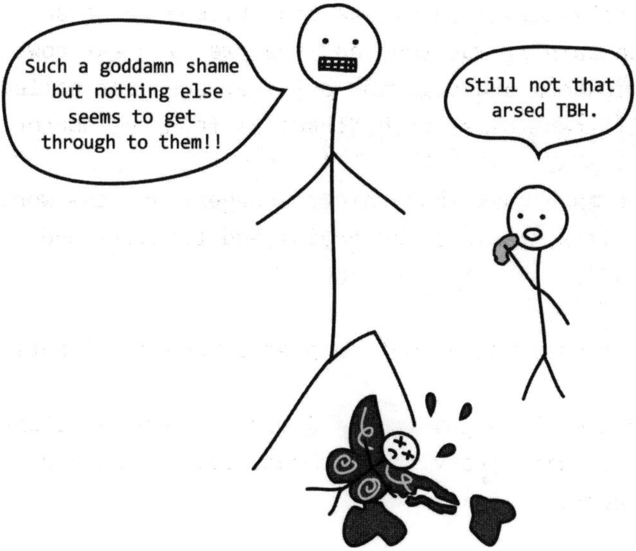
Such a goddamn shame but nothing else seems to get through to them!!
Still not that arsed TBH.

THURSDAY, 26 OCTOBER

Still no joy in getting rid of Chase. Amelie said she had some more ideas we could put into place if things get desperate.

FRIDAY, 27 OCTOBER

I've told Mummy that I've become a vegetable because eating chicken is mean and uncalled for. She said that I might find it a bit difficult seeing as I don't like any actual vegetables.

Just my luck that all the foods that used to be animals are my favourites. The one good thing is that pesto pasta is apparently not dead body parts.

SATURDAY, 28 OCTOBER

My first day of being a vegetable!

6.47 a.m. Eat Coco Pops. This is easy.

9.01 a.m. Daddy announces he is having bacon for breakfast.

9.23 a.m. Can smell bacon cooking.

9.24 a.m.–9.26 a.m. Caught in moral dilemma.

9.27 a.m. Starving. Decide to start eating dead animals again. I feel sad for them and all but at the end of the day my attention span is too short to realistically give a shit.

SUNDAY, 29 OCTOBER

Clocks went back in the night so my official get-up time was 3.39 a.m. There'll be almost no point in going to bed in the first place soon, which would suit me quite well as I don't really get the point of sleeping anyhow.

MONDAY, 30 OCTOBER

Went to Tesco to choose our Halloween costumes,
picked out pumpkin ones for me and Chase. Very
excited to wear them tomorrow.

TUESDAY, 31 OCTOBER - HALLOWEEN

Decided I looked like an absolute twat in my pumpkin costume so refused to put it on. Mummy insisted I let her at least take a photo - I reluctantly agreed and was absolutely mortified to discover she then posted it on Facebook.

This is a total invasion of our privacy and I will sue her arse off for this when I am big enough to have some money.

👍 Like   💬 Comment   ➤ Share

👍 ❤️ 😊 37 people like this

Oh what grumpy little pumpkins!!

Cruel Mummy!

Later on we went out trick-or-treating, which is basically knocking on random people's doors and asking for sweets. Amazing – why don't we do this all year?

The only issue I had was that when we got home Mummy said I could only eat two of my sweets – yep, you read that right . . . two of MY sweets.

Apparently it was already late and eating E-numbers before bed is never a good idea because they are bad for your teeth and make it hard for you to sleep.

I kind of see where she's coming from but obviously I'm not going to sleep tonight anyway . . . there are scary monsters and ghosts out there!!

WEDNESDAY, 1 NOVEMBER – AKA MY BIRTHDAY MONTH

I'm not so arrogant that I'm going to go on about it every single day but I WAS BORN IN NOVEMBER!!!!

I cannot wait for my party – I have been thinking long and hard about the theme and have decided it will be *Paw Patrol* and Bing Bunny mash-up with a hint of the Jurassic era for good measure.

THURSDAY, 2 NOVEMBER

Apparently as I was born on the 25th it is still quite a long time until my birthday and going on about it every five seconds is not going to make it happen quicker. Le sigh.

SUNDAY, 5 NOVEMBER

I have tried and failed to make sense of the horror I have just endured . . .

They took me to a freezing cold field in the middle of the night; they said it was a treat.

There was a dead body in a wheelbarrow, and people were pushing it around and laughing!

Crowds of people stuffed cheap-looking meat products into their faces. The smell of burning flesh filled the air. There was a HUGE fire and no sign of anyone trying to extinguish it!

'CALL FIREMAN SAM!' I shouted. But everyone just stood there doing nothing – they seemed to be enjoying it!

Then, without warning, huge explosions filled the air, BANG BANG BANG BANG BANG! Is this the end of civilisation, I thought?!

Then I watched in disgust as they took the body,
I believe he was a chap named Guy, and threw him
mercilessly to the flames - CHEERING AS HE BURNED!

What is this sick world we live in?!

MONDAY, 6 NOVEMBER

An interesting conversation with Mummy when she was having a shower today . . .

Me: Mummy don't have a willy!

Mummy: No, that's right, I don't.

Me: How does Mummy get wees out then?

Mummy: Well, er, there is a . . . little hole.

Me: Mummy has a hole?!

TUESDAY, 7 NOVEMBER

At circle time today I asked Jasmine if she had a willy or a hole and she went all red like a tomato.

WEDNESDAY, 8 NOVEMBER

Apparently I was being a total dickhead today. #WinningAtLife

THURSDAY, 9 NOVEMBER

Dearest Mummy,

I've noticed lately that you've changed. I've seen you trying to exert some sort of authority over me and almost believing that you've done it. Well . . . er . . . you so haven't.

You might think that I am not fully wise to the tricks you are using to indoctrinate me into this 'ideological world', but what do you think we talk about all day at nursery? Only the other day I was regaling my crew with your predictable tactics! It seems you need it spelling out . . .

No pudding
I may have eaten all my tea for a lousy fromage frais if I hadn't already pilfered two custard creams and a chocolate Hobnob. FYI I am growing upwards towards the biscuit tin.

Bribery

I know that every time we go out for a meal you fill your handbag with treats. I also know that I don't need to behave to get them, in fact firing cutlery at people's heads is much more effective. I see that look of desperation in your eyes and we all know what desperation means, don't we? Yeh – lollipops. AND there's no point even trying to bluff that you don't have any, cos, well . . . let's just say I've been undoing your handbag zips since 2016.

The naughty step

How can you possibly think spending three minutes sitting on a step is a suitable punishment for playing British Bulldog with the cat? You see, the naughty step is what you make it – I can sing, chat gibberish, laugh hysterically to myself. Sometimes if I'm bored I might just empty a box of cereal on the floor and go and sit on it myself – you are so easy to wind up!

Confiscation *(AKA stealing my screen time) HOW VERY DARE YOU?! Unboxing videos = life. After last time you know not to go here again, don't you?!*

Remember – you can take away our YouTube access BUT YOU WILL NEVER TAKE OUR FREEDOM!!!!

Shouting

This is my favourite as we both know you have totally lost it at this point! I feel particularly proud of myself if I manage to break you down in public as other people's disapproving stares really are the icing on the cake. To top it all off it usually ends in an apology from YOU for your bad parenting! Ha ha!

So it's an E for effort and a big fat F for originality. I know you're better than this, please try harder.

Your ever-loving son,

Archie x

SUNDAY, 12 NOVEMBER

Oh dear, the Father Christmas threats have already started - a new record, methinks!

It is November.
This person is an idiot.

MONDAY, 13 NOVEMBER

Get this. Went to playgroup today and this utter chancer pushed his Chicco baby walker right into Chase and made her cry.

From absolutely nowhere I was engulfed by a sea of rage and put him well and truly in his place!

Mummy looked kind of proud and said I was learning what it was like to be a sibling. Apparently it's OK for you to be a bit mean to your little brother or sister but if anyone else does it then you just have to SOCK IT TO 'EM . . . because as Peggy Mitchell (RIP) used to say, 'We're faaaaaaamily!' And families stick together.

TUESDAY, 14 NOVEMBER

We made cress people at nursery last week and today we got to bring them home.

Mine is called Belinda and I love her SO much.

I find talking to her so therapeutic; we have the same opinions on everything, it's like we are soul mates.

WEDNESDAY, 15 NOVEMBER

Amelie's mum snipped all the hair off her cress person (George) and put it in her egg sandwich. Murdering bitch!

SATURDAY, 18 NOVEMBER

Went shopping at Aldi because Mummy heard it's trendy to be thrifty. Full of absolute reprobates!

The packing system at the tills was utter chaos. I thought Mummy was going to get punched.

I insisted we take my BFF Belinda EVERYWHERE. Mummy wasn't so keen – jealous, perhaps?

Belinda was left traumatised by the whole experience as she usually shops in Waitrose. She's classy like that.

The Aldi knock-off chocolate fingers are well good though.

SUNDAY, 19 NOVEMBER

Spent much of the day with Belinda, I really do not know what I would do without her. She is the only one who truly understands me.

Without her I might cease to exist.

MONDAY, 20 NOVEMBER

Everything felt like it was going a bit too
well today. Mummy told Daddy I'd been an utter
delight . . . say what?!?! I have a reputation to
uphold!

. . . So I drew a big picture of a knob in the
hallway to help restore the equilibrium.

TUESDAY, 21 NOVEMBER

BELINDA IS DEAD AND EVERYTHING IS RUINED.

They have been so busy taking care of Chase that they have forgotten to water her - it is now perfectly clear where their loyalties lie!

THURSDAY, 23 NOVEMBER

Mummy has apologised. Said she was a bit tired and dropped a ball. I'm tired! Tired of life! Why does no one care about me?

Daddy thought having a funeral for Belinda may help me process my grief so we took her remains out into the garden and gave her a proper send-off. Daddy said a few nice words and I held his hand as I sprinkled some Cheerios over her resting place. I think we all felt a bit better afterwards.

FRIDAY, 24 NOVEMBER

An ode to Belinda

My heart aches, my body full of pain,
How I long to see your perfect shell.
I liked you better than my best toy train,
My friend, my confidante, my belle.

You had a beautiful green head of hair,
And an enigmatic felt-tip face,
You understood me, you were always there,
YOU NEVER HAD A BABY AND THEN FORGOT I EVEN
FUCKING EXISTED.

And oh although our time was brief,
I won't forget a single leaf.
Though few, they were the best of days,
I vow I'll never eat egg and cress mayonnaise!

RIP Belinda. Nov 1997–Nov 1997.

SATURDAY, 25 NOVEMBER

5.11 a.m. I wake with a heavy heart. Today is my birthday but I feel little like celebrating in light of Belinda's needless passing.

5.13 a.m. For the sake of my party guests I must soldier on! Belinda was such a glass-half-full kind of girl – it is what she would have wanted. I shall go and wake everyone up for my present-opening ceremony.

5.23 a.m. I GOT A BIKE I GOT A BIKE I GOT A BIKE I GOT A BIKE I GOT A BIKE!!!! IT IS BEAUTIFUL AND SHINY AND BLUE AND IT HAS A BELL AND IT IS THE BEST BIKE IN THE WORLD EVER AND I HAVE THE BEST MUMMY AND DADDY IN THE UNIVERSE!!!

2.47 p.m. Had a bit of an episode earlier. Got so overexcited that I forgot I needed to breathe and started to hyperventilate. Daddy calmed me down and then we went out on my bike for six hours – what a wonderful day! Can't wait for my party later ☺

6.29 p.m. Well, that was bloody awful. I have several grievances so I decided to make a list:

- The theme was wrong. I changed my mind in my dreams last night and if anyone had bothered to read my mind they would have realised 'Galactic Postman Pat versus Power Rangers in the jungle' was my final decision.

- The props, accessories and tableware left a lot to be desired. Didn't they even bother creating a Pinterest board? It all just looked sort of 'whatever you could buy in Poundland' to me.

- We played 'pass the parcel' which seemed to be some sort of horrific ritual designed to torture young children. I mean, you get to hold a present and then you must give it away and watch someone else open it! How is this meant to be fun?!

- Tensions were already running high and then Sebastian won the main prize so I head-butted him. Obviously. Everything went downhill after that.

- The bouncy castle turned into some sort of battle scene from *Game of Thrones*. Amelie elbowed Poppy in the eye so Poppy ripped a chunk of Amelie's hair out and they both had to be taken home screaming.

- I was initially pleased with the cake but upon closer inspection it looked to be shop bought.

I mean you only turn three once – make a bit of bloody effort!

- They chopped up the aforementioned cake and gave it to other people to eat! Shop bought or not, it was MY cake! MINE.

- To add insult to injury the surviving guests were then given a bag of toys and sweets to take home with them – had they not had enough?! Should I have offered up a vial of my blood too?!

Feeling pretty violated right now, to be honest, with you. Next year I'm pinning this to the front door:

Dear Valued Party Guest,

Thank you for coming! Please leave your present at the front door and fuck off again.

Yours gratefully, Archie Adams

SUNDAY, 26 NOVEMBER

Suffering effects of the post-birthday comedown.
Can't quite cope with the sugar withdrawal; my
body is in spasm and I am doing bad things – I just
cannot seem to connect my mind with my conscience.
Perhaps I need an IV of liquidised Haribo?

Took my bike out to the park in the afternoon
and saw someone riding the same one but in red.
Decided I liked the red one better.

TUESDAY, 28 NOVEMBER

A discovery! After I go to bed, they do not ‘spend a bit of time tidying and cleaning before eating a vegetable-based dinner and following me up shortly after’, what they actually do is wait until I am asleep and then get a secret stash of good snacks out and stuff their faces with them in front of the telly! What an absolute sham!

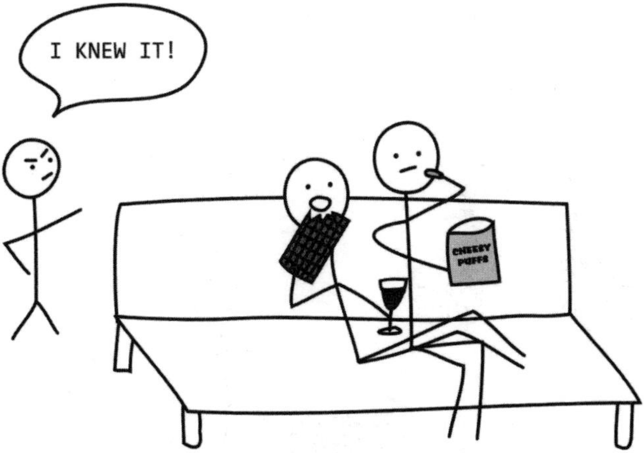
I KNEW IT!
CHEESY PUFFS

WEDNESDAY, 29 NOVEMBER

Since I've turned three I've definitely matured. My brain is so hungry for new information and I'm constantly seeking the answers to some of life's more crucial questions like 'How do snails work?', 'What do clouds do?' and 'Why do we need the sea?'

Luckily Mummy is very patient and really enjoys these Q&A sessions.

THURSDAY, 30 NOVEMBER

Something weird happened today. Chase smiled at me. I felt some strange feelings that I hadn't felt before – sort of warm and fuzzy. What kind of sorcery is this?! Am I beginning to weaken?

FRIDAY, 1 DECEMBER

Advent calendar day!!

I was so excited I think I may have possibly woken up before 4 a.m. It was freezing cold and dark but I didn't let that get in the way of seeing what was behind door one. A Christmas tree, in case you were interested. Mummy wasn't.

We have an Elf on the Shelf too. He watches me all the time to make sure I'm good, and when I'm sleeping he does naughty things around the house.

Today he was eating my Coco Pops! Would have been hilarious if seeing other people touch my breakfast cereal didn't make me all ragey. There will be hell to pay if I catch the creepy-looking motherfucker doing it again.

SATURDAY, 2 DECEMBER

Today Mummy and Daddy had their annual fight about Christmas trees. Daddy wanted a fake tree because they work out cheaper and are more practical; Mummy said fake trees are tacky and don't smell nice. Daddy said we'd be hoovering up pine needles for a year and it'd be half dead by Christmas; Mummy said, 'JUST GET ME A REAL TREE, YOU TIGHT GIT!'

So we went out and bought a massive one for £75 which Daddy said was 'daylight robbery!'

I asked them why people put trees in their living rooms anyway and no one seemed to have any idea. Maybe for kicking?

We spent the afternoon decorating the tree while everyone got slightly sozzled on mulled wine. It looked really great afterwards!

Later on I caught Mummy taking all the decorations off and doing it again. Bloody cheek of it.

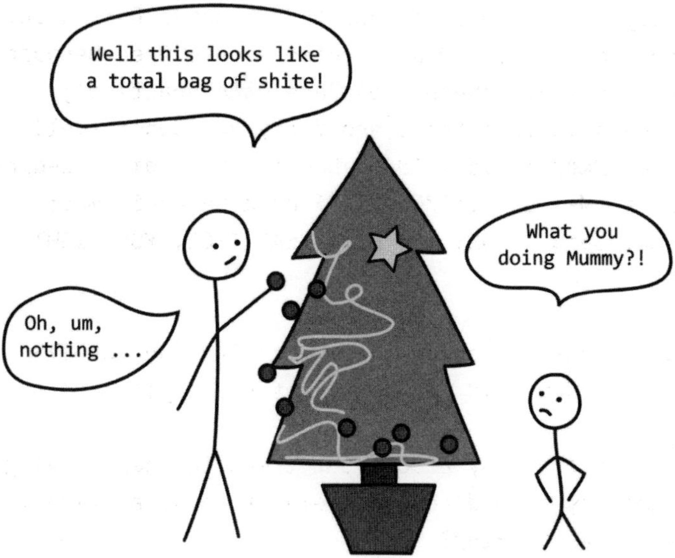
Well this looks like a total bag of shite!
What you doing Mummy?!
Oh, um, nothing ...

SUNDAY, 3 DECEMBER

Woke up and went downstairs to find the Elf just lying there on the kitchen table almost like someone had forgotten to move him - thought he might be dead so I screamed!

Mummy gave him CPR and luckily he was OK.

MONDAY, 4 DECEMBER

I accidentally ripped the door off my calendar in a frenzy to get to the chocolate. Am devastated, to put it mildly.

TUESDAY, 5 DECEMBER

Today Little Angels held auditions for the Nativity. It was a bit like *X Factor* Bootcamp but way more savage.

WEDNESDAY, 6 DECEMBER

So, so sick of this 'one door a day!' malarkey.
Who makes all these stupid rules anyway?!

THURSDAY, 7 DECEMBER

Fuck the system!

Got up at 5.15 a.m. and opened all of my doors and
ate all of the chocolate. It felt SO good!

Mummy and Daddy were quite cross. They said I've
ruined it for myself and not to blame them when I
wake up tomorrow morning with no doors to open.

FRIDAY, 8 DECEMBER

Woke up and there was no door to open. So cross at Mummy and Daddy for allowing this to happen, they should know that I am too young to take responsibility for my own actions.

SATURDAY, 9 DECEMBER

Today we went to meet Father Christmas. I thought he lived in the North Pole but it turns out it's actually Greenacres Garden Centre. Curious.

I was really excited when we were queuing up but when I got into his magical grotto (which actually just looked like a shed full of polystyrene balls) Mummy said I should go and sit on his knee for a photo, but he smelt a bit like whisky and fags so I didn't want to.

I asked him for a Nerf gun but when I excitedly unwrapped the present he gave me it was a tub of poxy Play-Doh. FML.

Got really cross, started kicking off and 'causing a scene'. All the other parents were staring so Mummy told them I was 'just a bit tired and overwhelmed', which was rubbish because if anything I was completely underwhelmed, or totally lacking in any kind of whelm at all. It was just all a bit disappointingly crap!

SUNDAY, 10 DECEMBER

They did it to us again.

Spent the afternoon googling the process of parental emancipation.

👍 Like 💬 Comment ➤ Share

👍 💜 😊 44 people like this

PMSL. One to keep for their wedding days! ;)

Gorgeous wee puds!

MONDAY, 11 DECEMBER

The Elf hadn't moved again! Mummy said maybe he was feeling a little bit poorly and perhaps it would be easier if he just sat on the mantelpiece for the rest of December to see if that helps him regain some strength.

TUESDAY, 12 DECEMBER

Jasmine revealed our parts for the Nativity. I am playing the very important part of Sheep 3. I only have one line, 'BAAAAAAAAAAA!', which I say just after Jesus gets born. It's pretty integral so I've been practising loads in front of the mirror.

Amelie got the part of Mary, which was a massive relief as she said she was going to burn the place down if Sophia got it.

WEDNESDAY, 13 DECEMBER

The incident in Tesco today wasn't really my fault - I was suffering from dehydration and needed a Fruit Shoot for survival purposes. I find water just doesn't revive me quick enough when I am in such a weak, semi-catatonic state.

Mummy keeps threatening that if I don't start behaving better then Father Christmas won't come. He even called me up on her phone to say I'd been put on the naughty list. #Jobsworth

THURSDAY, 14 DECEMBER

Amelie said Mummy is bullshitting me again and that it wasn't really Father Christmas, just an automated app on her phone.

Not convinced Amelie is right – the dude knew my name and everything!

FRIDAY, 15 DECEMBER

Dear Father Christmas,

I have been a REALLY good boy this year (anyone who tells you otherwise is lying or drunk). I am slightly worried you may be getting some negative feedback on my behaviour from unreliable sources so I have put together a few useful quotes from non-biased parties.

Jasmine (my keyworker at nursery) — 'Really helpful, great at tidy-up time, loves crafting and never bites, a real team player!'

Mr Fluffy (my cat) — 'A gentle and loving pet owner. Likes grooming me and never tries to ride me.'

Amelie (best friend) — 'Archie's parents clearly love his little sister much more than him but he has dealt with the overwhelming favouritism with total decorum and maturity and never once tried to hurt her — a true hero!'

Glad we've got that cleared up! So please could I have . . .

1. *Pages 115–128 (inclusive) of the Toys R Us catalogue*

2. *An unlimited supply of Tangfastics*

3. *An iPhone 7 Plus with 128GB storage and 25GB data*

4. *An all-inclusive holiday to Adventure Bay to meet the Paw Patrol crew*

5. *A yellow Lamborghini Gallardo*

6. *A driving licence (see above)*

7. *3-foot roll of bubble wrap*

8. *My own credit card*

9. *My little sister to be sent to live with a new family in Tasmania*

Love, Archie Adams x

P.S. Nice to meet you at the garden centre the other day. Sorry about the way I reacted, it was just that you smelt like Daddy after a night out and it was a bit shocking TBH. I understand everyone needs to let their hair down once in a while, though – especially you!

SATURDAY, 16 DECEMBER

I have a new game to play. It's called 'baby buckaroo' and you basically cover the baby in as many household objects as you can until you get caught and reprimanded. Much fun.

TUESDAY, 19 DECEMBER

The Nativity is tomorrow so we had a full dress rehearsal today. Amelie refused to remove her unicorn horn and Jasmine said if she wouldn't take it off then she'd have to give the part of Mary to Sophia.

Long story short, her reaction wasn't great and Amelie is now Shepherd 2 and absolutely livid about it. She has to wear a tea towel on her head, which she says is beneath her. Apparently unicorns would never wear tea towels as they are much too glamorous for that!

I don't know why they were making such a big deal out of it anyway – the whole Nativity story already sounds ridiculously far-fetched to me. Mary also happening to be a magical unicorn surely doesn't make that much difference?

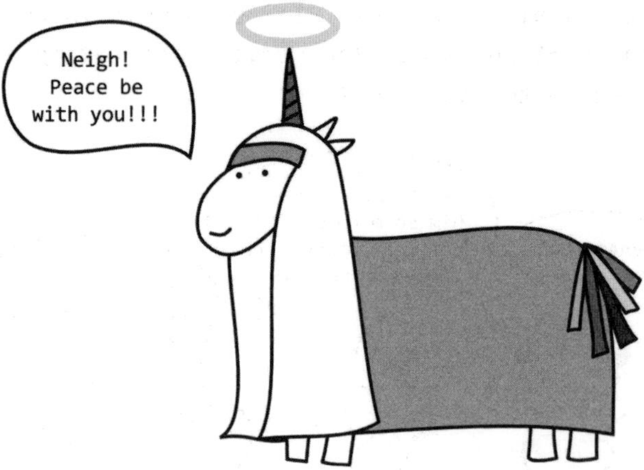
Neigh! Peace be with you!!!

WEDNESDAY, 20 DECEMBER

So it was all going well, I looked good in my sheep outfit and Mummy kept crying and taking pictures - the daft cow!

Then suddenly Amelie went absolutely batshit. Grabbed baby Jesus, tried to throw him at Sophia, missed and hit Noah who was playing Balthazar – it boshed him in the nose – blood EVERYWHERE . . . all over Jesus! Looked more like a scene out of *Lord of the Flies* than the Nativity.

SATURDAY, 23 DECEMBER

Daddy was right – the tree already looks half dead.

He keeps on getting the vacuum cleaner out and tutting while hoovering up the needles with a smug look on his face.

Mummy said the one good thing to come out of it is that he now knows where the vacuum cleaner is actually located. Touché.

SUNDAY, 24 DECEMBER

So apparently we saw 'Father Christmas' fly overhead. It would have been a bit more magical had all the adults not kept using the terms 'sleigh' and 'International Space Station' interchangeably and nudging each other and laughing when they got it wrong. Lesson one: most things about Christmas are utter bollocks.

Before I went to bed we left a plate out with snacks for Father Christmas and the reindeer. FC got a packet of Quavers and a G&T – apparently Daddy had eaten all the mince pies, the fat bastard. The reindeer food looked suspiciously like Go-Cat with glitter sprinkled over the top but who am I to question it?!

MONDAY, 25 DECEMBER – CHRISTMAS DAY

5.05 a.m. I rushed downstairs and to my extreme relief saw that HE had been. It seems the repeated threats of ending up on the naughty list didn't amount to much.

MENTAL NOTE: Next year don't let their 'he's always watching' bullshit influence your behaviour. Either he didn't see me doing the massive knob drawing in the hallway or he didn't give a rat's arse.

6.02 a.m. Had chocolate coins for breakfast. #FeelingAwesome

10.17 a.m. Just got back from Jesus's birthday party which, if I'm honest, sucked. No games, no cake, you weren't even supposed to dance when they did the singing! Also, if they don't like people repeatedly shouting 'IS IT TIME TO GO HOME NOW?' then why the hell do they ring a bell every five seconds? So confusing.

11.32 a.m. Granny came over with Auntie Mandy, Uncle Dave, the cousins and Great Auntie Ivy for PRESENT-OPENING TIME! I adopted my usual smash-and-grab approach. Basically, open everything as quickly as possible and if you don't like it throw it across the room; if you do like it say, 'WOW!' and then throw it across the room. Chase AKA 'lamebrain' got some cool stuff but just preferred looking at Christmas tree baubles. I didn't get much off my list – sadly Lamborghinis are a bit out of FC's price range, the penny-pinching old scrooge.

After we'd opened everything Daddy enjoyed helping us put our new toys together.

2.37 p.m. Lunch was ridiculous – too much of it, too many courses. It only takes me about eight seconds to eat my two mouthfuls so I have no idea why they would expect me to sit there and look happy with a ridiculous paper hat on my head while everyone else does that whole 'enjoying a nice meal' rubbish.

4.47 p.m. I mean they say that Christmas is for kids but it has become abundantly clear to me that Christmas is actually about busying your kids with new toys and then ignoring them while you get pissed.

Everyone seems quite battered now. If I complain about anything they just lob more chocolate coins at me – Best. Day. Ever.

6.17 p.m. Fight! It was like a real live episode of *EastEnders*. Mummy and Auntie Mandy were shouting at each other. Auntie Mandy has always thought she's better than Mummy, apparently. Not true – she looks like a horse! Daddy decided to bring up Brexit, Great Auntie Ivy started saying, 'I'm not being racist but in my day . . .' Full-on war broke out! Uncle Dave suggested a game of Cranium to diffuse the situation. Unfortunately he'd forgotten how competitive Mummy can get, especially after a few sherbets.

7.37 p.m. Everyone has gone. Polished off a handful of Quality Street and a chocolate Father Christmas for dinner. Mummy's having a little sleep on the sofa. Me and Daddy are watching *The Snowman* and I feel all Christmassy and magical. Love my life.

8.12 p.m. Mr Fluffy is shitting glitter – I knew it!!

THURSDAY, 28 DECEMBER

Everyone seems quite confused as to what to do with themselves or what day of the week it even is – over the last few days the activities on offer seem to consist of:

A. Going out for a nice winter walk.

B. Going to the pub.

C. Going out for a nice winter walk culminating in a trip to the pub.

D. Watching Christmas telly while stuffing your face with cheese, oven snacks and chocolate-orange segments and deluding yourself that you will go hard-core Paleo in January.

(D is a firm family favourite.)

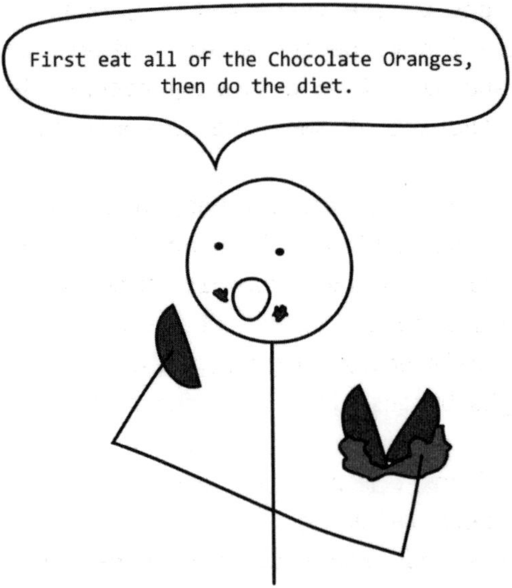
First eat all of the Chocolate Oranges, then do the diet.

SUNDAY, 31 DECEMBER

The last day of the year! And wow, what a year it has been – I have become a big brother, learned to shit and piss into a singing receptacle and mastered the art of swearing in context.

Apparently today is the day that we all make our New Year's resolutions, which are the things you're going to do to improve yourself. Mummy always digs out her leisurewear, dusts off the NutriBullet and declares she's going to give up the booze – everyone just laughs because they know she can't cut it!

Anyway, I know I'm pretty close to being perfect but I've been thinking of ways I can be a more considerate and altruistic person next year!

1. Be nicer to Mr Fluffy. He doesn't like being ridden on and that's his prerogative.

2. Stop licking things – especially bins, toilets and random people in the post office queue.

3. Consider wearing normal-people clothing rather than my default options of superheroes or nudity.

4. Learn to accept Chase. If attempts to sell her, murder her and put her up for adoption did not work then she is probably here to stay.

5. Listen to my body more. Give it what it's asking for – namely Fruit Shoots and Tangfastics. #SoWeak #SendSugar

6. The early bird catches the worm! Always get up by 5 a.m. (latest) thereby maximising the quality time we have together as a family.

7. Stop pissing myself because I'm having far too much fun to go to the toilet.

8. Think – is it really worth going batshit crazy because someone else looked at my scooter? Actually . . . bad example . . . that would be totally justified, but you know just perhaps try and be a bit more tolerant of other people's rude and uncouth behaviour.

9. Stop hiding food in my pants. It's smelly, unhygienic and it doesn't taste as good when you eat it later.

10. Try to start the day in a positive mood. It's not Mummy's fault that she continually messes up my breakfast, despite me telling her approximately 1,237 times how to do it properly. Have made her a handy guide to save further embarrassment . . .

Toddler Breakfast Planning Tool

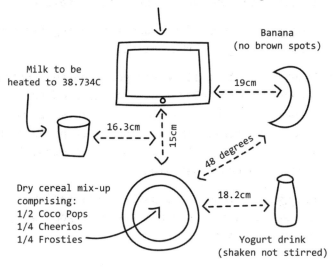

iPad to catch up on the CBeebies HQ morning news

Banana
(no brown spots)

Milk to be
heated to 38.734C

19cm

16.3cm

15cm

48 degrees

Dry cereal mix-up
comprising:
1/2 Coco Pops
1/4 Cheerios
1/4 Frosties

18.2cm

Yogurt drink
(shaken not stirred)

N.B. No cutlery required,
will eat directly with face

MONDAY, 1 JANUARY 2018 – NEW YEAR'S DAY

2.43 a.m. They came and got me out of bed just before midnight (they had clearly been drinking, which had led them to the opinion that it would be a good idea) because apparently they wanted to see in the New Year with me – Mummy said I was her 'best boy in the whole world!' IYF, Daddy!!!

Then once I was fully wound up and wired they tried to get me to go back to sleep! I think they probably ended up regretting it when I was still awake two and a quarter hours later but I had a great time, so whatevs.

I shall reward them for this rare treat by sleeping in for an extra four minutes tomorrow.

TUESDAY, 2 JANUARY

Everything has gone downhill. There are no more presents and we have to eat actual food again instead of foraging for chocolate on the Christmas tree. Who the hell do they think they are, just turning the tap off like that?!

As punishment I got all of my new toys out of their boxes, mixed them up into a big soupy mess and then played with my old toys.

Apparently 'There is too much crap in this house!' and I agree, they do need to get rid of some things – furniture, beds, whatever. Just as long as they don't touch any of my stuff, which is all absolutely VITAL.

WEDNESDAY, 3 JANUARY

Amelie came to nursery in her new Christmas present today – a pink electric Range Rover with alloy wheels and MP3 player. How come Father Christmas got her such a good present when I only got some Playmobil and a painting set?!?!

THURSDAY, 4 JANUARY

Mummy asked if we could sort through some of my old toys and dressing-up outfits and put them aside for charity. Apparently some children aren't as lucky as me and don't have as many things to play with. Sorry, er . . . how is this my problem?! NO WAY.

9.29 p.m. Finding it difficult to sleep – lots of noises and rustling going on downstairs. Hmmmmm.

FRIDAY, 5 JANUARY

Saw Lucy in the street. She's doing dry January too and is running a half-marathon in February.

I don't know why everyone attempts dry January anyway. I mean, look out of the window – it's bloody miserable out there. Have another drink, do what you've got to do to get through it FFS.

SATURDAY, 6 JANUARY

Well done, Mummy — she lasted five days! Not sure why she even bothers. She doesn't need to make excuses TBH, everyone's allowed a vice and we love her for the little wine-guzzler she is.

SUNDAY, 7 JANUARY

Mummy has been deceitful. She was looking in the cupboard under the stairs for some kitchen roll and I spied a bag of MY TOYS in there. WTF does she think she is doing?!

Went proper crazy. Demanded to look inside. Get this . . . full of all my Happy Meal toys, odd bits of jigsaws that I never did, scrunched-up pieces of *CBeebies* magazine, broken crayons – basically all my favourite stuff!! How very dare she!

To pay her back I went on a clearing spree of my own and collected all of the things that Mummy 'doesn't really need any more' like her Touche Éclat, toothbrush, car keys, diary, tampons, Chanel N°5, etc. etc. It was a bit predictable to put them in my usual hiding places like the bin or chucking them out of the bedroom window, so I went with the freezer.

MONDAY, 8 JANUARY

Tee hee hee, what a laugh. Took her an hour and a half to find everything.

TUESDAY, 9 JANUARY

A tragic event has occurred — Mr Fluffy has died!

It was all quite exciting really. It was a hit and run just outside our house. I saw the dead body and I think I even saw a bit of brain!

I wondered if it would be bad taste to include a picture, but I've done it anyway.

Mummy said I shouldn't be too upset as he was fourteen and had had a 'good innings' and it would probably save us quite a lot in vet's bills this way round. I'm sort of varying between being really upset and absolutely fascinated by the whole thing.

WEDNESDAY, 10 JANUARY

Started getting a bit worried about the concept of death. Why does everyone I love die? Mr Fluffy, Belinda, James Pond and Leonardo DiCarprio (Granny's koi carp), Mufasa, King Agnarr and Queen Iduna of Arendelle (I don't even like *Frozen* but it was still bloody sad!), Nemo's mum . . . Grandad!

I asked Mummy what would happen to Mr Fluffy now he was dead and she said he would go up to cat heaven and have a lovely life with all his old neighbourhood pals like Dave and Zorro and Mr Bojangles.

I pointed out he actually hated Mr Bojangles and she said yes, Mr Bojangles would probably go to hell in light of his mass-murder of an entire blackbird family in 2015.

Then we looked out of the window and Mummy pointed at the brightest, shiniest star and said that was 'probably Mr Fluffy'. Felt better.

THURSDAY, 11 JANUARY

Popped into Sainsbury's Local on the way back from nursery and Mummy bought me a Kinder Surprise to help cheer me up and a bottle of gin to help cheer herself up.

Opened my egg when I got home and it had a jigsaw in it. FML.

Found out today is called 'Blue Monday', the most depressing day of the entire year. Figures.

It never rains but it pours.

FRIDAY, 12 JANUARY

Amelie came over for a play at ours and I told her I had seen Mr Fluffy as a beautiful star in the sky and she said that was all a load of rubbish and that stars are just a bunch of hot gas floating about in space and when we die it is FOREVER and there is nothing at all except OBLIVION and even more NOTHINGNESS.

11.55 p.m. BAD DREAMS!

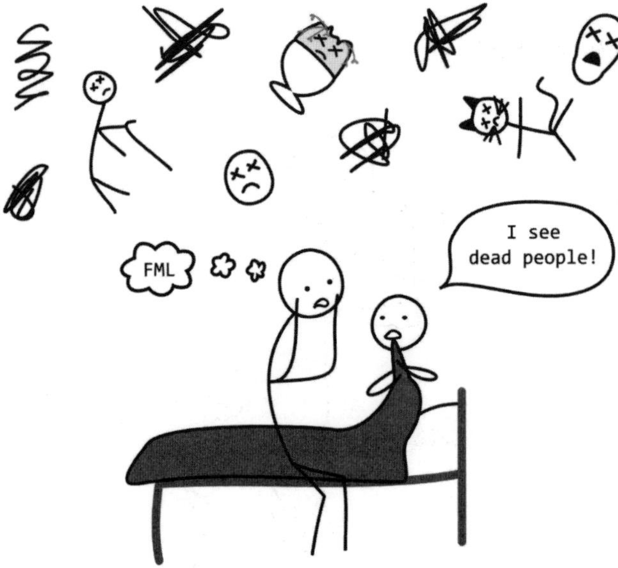
FML
I see dead people!

SATURDAY, 13 JANUARY

Too weak to write much. Me and Chase have been struck down with some sort of horrific vomiting bug! It's like something out of *The Exorcist*.

So. Much. Sick.

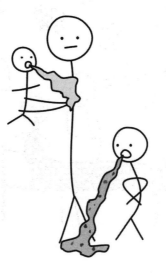

SUNDAY, 14 JANUARY

00.11 a.m. Chase is sick.

00.47 a.m. I am sick.

01.55 a.m. Chase is sick.

02.39 a.m. I am sick.

03.03 a.m. I do a shit that explodes through my night-time nappy pants.

04.12 a.m. Me and Chase are simultaneously cry-vomiting. Vomit comes out of my nose. I accidentally rub it through my hair in the panic and then I am sick on Chase's head.

05.33 a.m. We have a hose-down in the bath. There is no more clean bedding so we move to Mummy and Daddy's bed.

06.24 a.m. OH MY LIFE – Daddy is down!

07.17 a.m. Mummy is down too!! But wait, what is this? She's just carrying on!! For Mummy, being sick almost looks like she's normal – what a legend!

MONDAY, 15 JANUARY

Death stares me in the face!

At least I have left this diary as my everlasting legacy. Whoever shall find it please publish it and donate all the profits to the preservation of Crazy Monkey's Fun Palace.

I shall end with a quote from Shakespeare . . .

To die, to sleep;
To sleep: perchance to dream: ay, there's the rub;
For in that sleep of death what dreams may come
When we have shuffled off this mortal coil,
Must give us pause: there's the respect
That makes calamity of so long life.
(*Hamlet*, Act III, Scene I)

I have absolutely zero idea what the chuff he is on about but he's meant to be dead clever, like, and I couldn't think of anything better.

Goodbye, sweet life ☹

TUESDAY, 16 JANUARY

Phew — back from the brink! Still feeling weak so spent the day watching TV. Some observations:

- Elvis is a complete moron, the Station Officer Steele/Trevor/Dilys love triangle makes me want to heave and the whole town of Pontypandy and everyone in it would have burnt to a crisp if it weren't for Fireman Sam who, yes, is a hero, but is also a despicable maintenance-payment-dodger for denying parentage of his bastard son Norman Price.

- Thomas is not a 'really useful engine'. He is a total liability.

- What is Topsy and Tim's mum on? Opiates?!

- *In the Night Garden* is utter filth. The Tombliboos need to learn to keep their trousers on, Upsy Daisy needs to stop dragging her bed around and constantly exposing herself to Igglepiggle, Makka Pakka is some sort of anti-social pervert who lives alone and is obsessed with polishing his pebbles, and the Pontipines and the Wottingers need a good solid lesson in contraception!

- Why the fuck is the deputy mayor of Adventure Bay a sodding chicken?!

- Is it our taxes that are paying for the Octonauts to jaunt about the ocean on a seemingly endless mission to save injured fish and emotionally wounded crustaceans?! And who the frick came up with the concept of ping-pong playing, cake-baking, fish/vegetable hybrid people called 'Vegimals'?! Were the writers of this show taking LSD?

- Mr Tumble's whole family looks suspiciously inbred if you ask me.

- I find the fact that Bing Bunny is looked after by a small knitted character (relationship unspecified) called Flop very creepy. Why is he so tiny? What even is he? A sock monkey gone wrong?!

- I don't even know where to begin with the carnival of hell that is *Waybuloo*. Is it supposed to be relaxing? Because it's actually terrifying! To top it off, they can't even speak properly. It's not 'Me not like it', Lau Lau! It's 'I DON'T FUCKING LIKE IT!'

THURSDAY, 18 JANUARY

Everyone is fine now. Except for Daddy. Daddy seems to have been affected worst of all and he is still just lying in bed, weak and helpless.

SATURDAY, 20 JANUARY

I'm still having a lot of trouble sleeping. What with the horrific drive-by killing of Mr Fluffy and my own near-death experience I am terrified to be left alone.

Mummy is being incredibly kind and patient as usual, though. She sits with me stroking my head and singing sweet lullabies until I finally drift off. I don't know what I'd do without her.

MONDAY, 22 JANUARY

Lucy came round today. She told Mummy she looked tired – the dick!

Mummy told her that Chase still wakes up twenty-seven times a night so yes, she was actually a wee bit tired, and Lucy proceeded to offer her a variety of unsolicited parenting advice because her ugly Ewok baby sleeps for thirteen hours and gets up at 8.30 a.m.

Apparently she's loving every second of 'mumdom' and finds it very sad that so many mums are always whinging about their kids!

She obviously didn't see Mummy's Facebook post from this morning when she threatened to leave me and Chase in a lay-by.

THURSDAY, 25 JANUARY

Today I opened my lunchbox to find that my sandwiches had been cut into squares instead of triangles. So uncouth.

Honestly, how am I meant to live like this?!?

In contrast Imogen was proudly eating a peanut butter sandwich that her mum had cut into the shape of a diplodocus — she must think I'm an absolute heathen!

SATURDAY, 27 JANUARY

This morning I saw Mummy looking in the mirror and she seemed really sad.

I heard her say to Daddy that she wasn't sure she was a very good mum and that other people (who?!) seemed to be doing a better job than her (not true), that she shouted too much (possibly true) and that everyone else's kids ate vegetables and didn't piss in their parents' shoes (debatable).

She said she felt dowdy and fat (say what?!) and wishes she was more like Lucy. (I BLOODY WELL DON'T!)

I don't get it. I wonder why she can't see what we see?!

SUNDAY, 28 JANUARY

I think I've worked out the answer to my earlier
quandary re. what is the actual point of Daddy?

Daddy (noun):
*The one we take the piss out of, the one who
sometimes gets forgotten, the one who makes us
laugh, the one who is quietly keeping us all
together.*

TUESDAY, 30 JANUARY

A new boy called Hugo has started at Little Angels.

Amelie seems quite taken with him and at lunchtime she gave him my seat – we always sit next to each other!

It was all Hugo this and Hugo that . . . apparently his was the best Modified Cobra she'd ever seen – then she let him try on her horn!

Am heartbroken. Must up my game tomorrow.

WEDNESDAY, 31 JANUARY

Arrived at nursery today wearing my best clothes (Iron Man padded muscle suit, Batman cape, Optimus Prime mask and Paw Patrol wellies).

Hugo was already there, playing with Amelie; he was wearing fairy wings and a pink wig and he looked like a total twat.

Amelie said she really liked that he was such a 'modern man' and didn't conform to the gender stereotypes imposed on us by the patriarchy. Got really angry and hit Hugo on the head with a mallet I'd fashioned out of Duplo.

Mummy was very cross to hear of my violent outburst at pick-up time. She said jealousy was not a very nice trait and when good things happen to other people you should try and be happy for them.

Confused! Didn't see her being very happy for Lucy when she had her drug-free, unassisted water birth!

THURSDAY, 1 FEBRUARY

Amelie and Hugo are boyfriend and girlfriend. They didn't waste any time, did they? The pair of brazen hussies!

Tried to take Mummy's advice and feel happy for them but I just couldn't do it. My overriding feeling is that I would like Hugo to burn in the fiery pits of hell!

I will just have to accept that perhaps I'm not a very nice person.

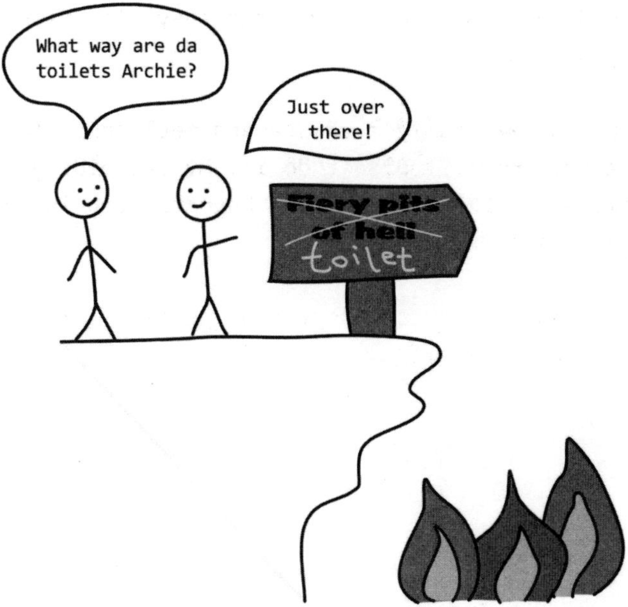
What way are da toilets Archie?
Just over there!
~~Fiery pits of hell~~
toilet

FRIDAY, 2 FEBRUARY

Went to the park. Started eating the sand, just because . . . I dunno - just did. It was a right fucker to get out of my mouth. Started spitting and screaming and hitting Mummy because I was sure it was her fault . . . somehow. What should I do about all of these uncontrollable violent outbursts I keep having?! Who knows . . . I barely know myself any more!

MONDAY, 5 FEBRUARY

Went with Mummy to drop a parcel round to Lucy's house, rang the bell and guess what we found!! Lucy standing there in her PJ bottoms and a big sick stain on her top - looking godawful.

She took us through to the kitchen and there was mess everywhere!!! She was dead embarrassed and said she'd just got back from the McDonald's Drive-Thru and it was usually tidier than this and then looked like she was going to cry. Mummy said it was tidier than ours (which was a lie) and then Lucy actually did start crying while finishing her Big Mac and spluttering special sauce all over her chin.

She said she was sorry sometimes she was a bit of a bitch. She said she'd lied about the birth and she'd had ALL the drugs and it was horrendous and she hated it. She said she'd wondered why the baby was so ugly (told you!) and if she was ever going to look at it like people do in the adverts. She said that breastfeeding had been a disaster and that she'd been topping up with formula since day three and nearly all of her milk had now dried up. She said she feels like a big fat failure and it would all probably be OK if the baby EVER FUCKING SLEPT but it didn't. She said Gina Ford was a fucking liar and she'd spent £800 on a bespoke sleep consultation and it was all just a load of bollocks because the baby was nocturnal and probably actually a bat or a vampire or some sort of subhuman species that defies the laws of existence and just doesn't need to sleep. But she said she needed to sleep and if she didn't get some fucking sleep soon she was worried she was going to kill someone and once last week she took a golf club to the TV and smashed it in because she was delirious with tiredness and Piers Morgan seemed to be taunting her – but it didn't help at all and all it meant was that she also had to add ordering a new telly to her already ridiculously long to-do list.

Mummy poured Lucy a large glass of wine and told her that she was normal and that everyone probably felt a bit like doing that to the telly when Piers Morgan was on it (fair point).

And they talked a lot and even laughed a bit while
I ate the rest of the chips for my dinner (yum)
and then Mummy told Lucy to go and have a little
lie-down and she fell asleep almost right away.
I played on her iPad because of the smashed-up TV
situation and Mummy did the washing-up and looked
after the babies and when Lucy's husband Dan came
back, Mummy told him that Lucy wasn't perhaps
coping as well as she was making out and maybe she
needed a little bit of support and – get this –
Dan didn't even know! So he promised to sit down

and properly listen to her and work out ways that
he could help.

Then we left and went home and all I could think
was — wow, isn't my mummy a total hero!

. . . And also, why are adults so full of shit?!
Wouldn't it be so much better if they were all
just honest with each other?

TUESDAY, 6 FEBRUARY

They said they were taking me to the doctor. They made it sound fun but a cruel fate was awaiting me. They grasped my arms tightly to my sides before plunging a huge sharp instrument deep into my flesh. I screamed and they didn't even care – they just did it again on the other arm!

Little scratch?! Little fucking scratch?! The condescending bastards.

Then they gave me a sticker and a lollipop and said I was a brave soldier . . . like that would make it all OK?!?!?! It was nothing short of barbaric.

TBF the lolly was strawberry and pretty decent though.

THURSDAY, 8 FEBRUARY

It's Valentine's Day next week. Mummy says if you love someone you should tell them! She is helping me make a card for Amelie. I'm going to go head to head with Hugo to try to win her back. I will not take this lying down!

FRIDAY, 9 FEBRUARY

7.07 p.m. Mummy and Lucy have gone out on a Mums' night out – I tried various tricks to try and get her to stay but they didn't work: said I was poorly, said I was dying, screamed 'DON'T LEAVE ME MUMMY I LOVE YOU AND I NEVER GET TO SEE YOU, YOU HEARTLESS COW!!!' at her while she was doing her make-up. She was crying by the time Daddy pushed her out of the front door and told her that I'd be fine and that she should relax and have a good time.

I won't be fine – what the hell is he on about?! I have just been rejected by my own mother, who has chosen doing Jägerbombs over ME – HER SON!!

7.09 p.m. I'm fine. Daddy just gave me free rein on a family-size box of Maltesers. He's so awesome sometimes.

SATURDAY, 10 FEBRUARY

1.45 a.m. Woke up and heard some commotion outside. Looked out of the window and saw Mummy and Lucy outside (pretending to be dogs, perhaps?!). Think I might have preferred it when Mummy and Lucy didn't really like each other – watching two grown women crawl about on the pavement is pretty embarrassing. Felt deeply ashamed.

05.11 a.m. Set my internal body clock to wake up early in order to maximise my time with Mummy after last night's abandonment. Spent ten minutes staring at her beautiful face before defecating myself and letting the resulting stench rouse her from her sleep naturally. She woke up and screamed and then vomited. Bizarre.

1.27 p.m. We've done quite a lot of role-play games today. They mostly seem to involve Mummy pretending she has been critically injured in some way. I am the paramedic and my job is to attempt to resuscitate her while she lies on the sofa moaning.

3.13 p.m. Started feeling really bored. Daddy suggested Mummy might like to take me to soft play and Mummy looked like she was about to kill him. 'You've only got yourself to blame,' he said before Mummy threw the remote control at his winkle.

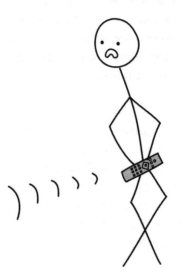

SUNDAY, 11 FEBRUARY

Mummy's feeling better — she said 'We must all get out for some fresh air!' which in her language means doing something middle-class old people do like visiting a National Trust property and looking at (not stomping on) all the nice (boring) flowers.

Daddy took his camera, which meant we were all instructed to look like we were having a lovely, wholesome day out so they could put it up on Facebook and pretend that we were normal. Sadly Chase and I wouldn't be party to their façade — I'm starting to think maybe me and little sis work pretty well as a team.

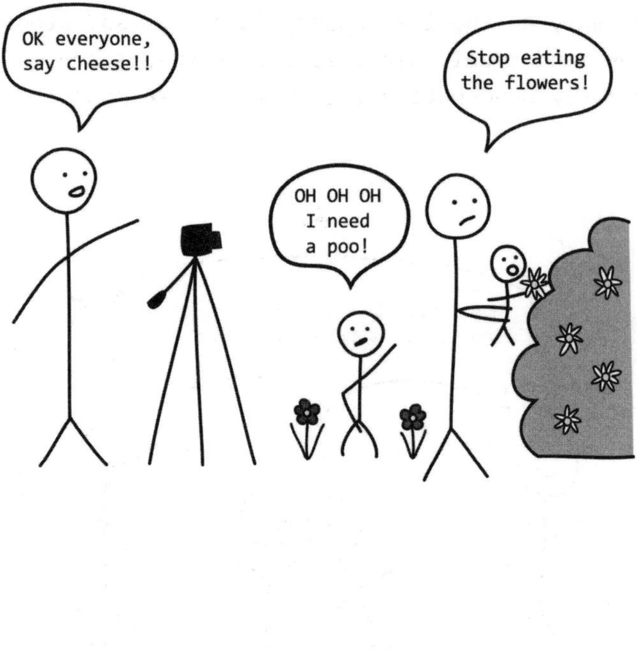
OK everyone, say cheese!!
OH OH OH I need a poo!
Stop eating the flowers!

MONDAY, 12 FEBRUARY

Playgroup this morning. They did Sleeping Bunnies twice at the end. Always a crowd-pleaser. This kid, must have been about two and a half, peaked too early on the last round, jumped up and stood on my hand really hard, like an actual stomp. I obviously head-butted the tosspot in response.

The outcome was we have been banned. Suits us all fine if I'm honest, as now we can just sit about in our PJs on Monday mornings – Mummy can watch *Homes under the Hammer* on the TV, I can watch *Fireman Sam* dubbed in German on her phone and Chase can just lie on her play mat sicking milk up and trying to work out how to roll. I've been helping her, she's nearly there! Advanced I reckon.

Playgroup is full of arseholes anyway.

TUESDAY, 13 FEBRUARY

Valentine's Day tomorrow. I have a feeling this
will be the making of me. Can't wait to give
Amelie my card!

WEDNESDAY, 14 FEBRUARY - VALENTINE'S DAY

Worst day of my life ever (apart from 8 November 2016 when I experimented with eating baked beans by inserting them into my nostrils). Amelie said she didn't want my card since she didn't believe in Valentine's Day as it was 'just a load of commercial bollocks!' She also said she was far too young to be thinking of settling down properly and that she wanted to sail the seven seas first and visit all the places her mummy has talked about like Kavos, Faliraki and Magaluf.

Cried all day!!

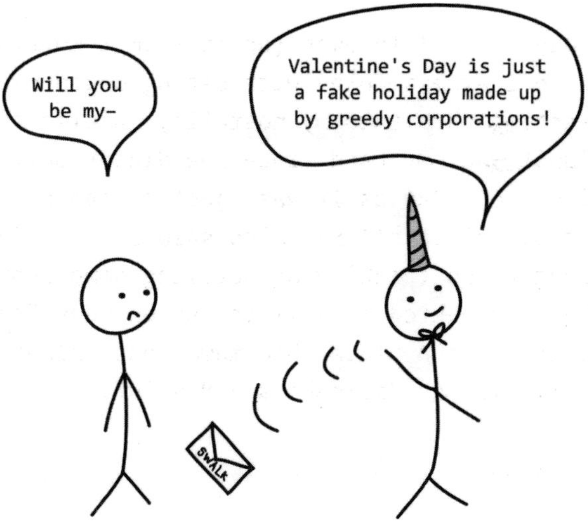
Will you be my-
Valentine's Day is just a fake holiday made up by greedy corporations!
SWALK

6.34 p.m. Realised what I should have known all along – that Mummy is my numero uno and I'll have plenty of time for girls when I'm older. So when I got home from nursery I gave her my card and she didn't even mind that I had crossed Amelie's name off because I couldn't be arsed to do a new one.

And for what it's worth (and it's worth everything), she said yes!

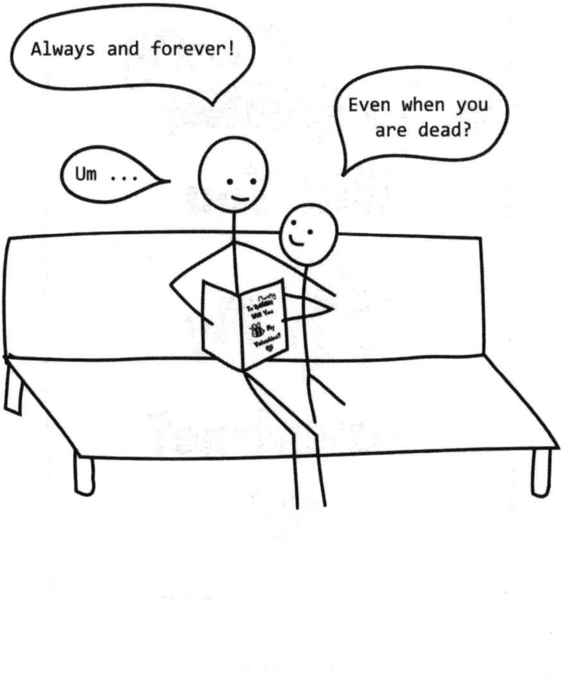
Always and forever!
Even when you are dead?
Um ...

THURSDAY, 15 FEBRUARY

12.06 a.m. Woke up due to strange noises. Got out of bed to investigate and found Mummy and Daddy doing the sexy time. Remembered what Amelie told me and put it into practice as I can't be going through all that again!

EPILOGUE

I've only got a couple of pages left so I'll have to leave you here. Daddy gave me a copy of the photo he took last Sunday and said I could stick it in my book . . .

My family

I don't think it came out quite how he'd hoped but I like it a lot . . . I mean Daddy might look like an utter buffoon, Mummy might look a bit ragey, I might *look* like I'm shitting my pants and Olivia . . . well she's just an idiot who likes eating flowers, so . . . BUT we are what we are and apparently that photo of our crazy, fighty, noisy, unhinged, imperfect family got 127 Facebook likes, which is a record for us! Perhaps being real is the new black?

Over and out,

Archie x

P.S. RIP Mr Fluffy, we really miss you!

ACKNOWLEDGMENTS

Firstly a big thank you to everyone who reads and supports me on the terrible, wonderful, confusing place that is the internet. It's so nice to have people attack the meanies for me so that I don't have to. Cheers for making me feel normal(ish).

To Charlotte, from that first email to two books done – mad! Thank you for your excellent guidance and support without which this book would have turned out to be a big murder fest.

To everyone at Hodder and Coronet, especially Emma, Alice, Fiona and Rosie for working so hard behind the scenes, and being such genuinely lovely people too.

To Jon and Millie for doing excellent agenty type things and, most importantly, making all the confusing stuff go away.

To Mum, Dad, Norman and Sheila for helping out with the boys and allowing me to actually have the time to write this bloody thing. Also, sorry about the swearing.

To Nicola, Hannah and Dawn, and their awesome offspring for the few snatched hours of extra childcare that #nakedclub brought. I miss those days already.

To Jim, for putting up with my breakdowns and frequent moments of self-doubt, and always reassuring me that I'm not actually being a crap mum/wife/general person. Oh and for plonking much appreciated glasses of wine down next to the laptop when I have my scowly face on.

To my boys who provide all the inspiration but are thankfully not quite as terrible as Archie! Well . . . you never used to bite anyone anyway ;)

You may frequently drive me round the bend but make me laugh like no one else can - I love the very bones of you.

Finally and most importantly to my De-Longhi fan heater whom I accidentally stole from letting agents that it would be wise not to publicly name. You keep my feet warm and toasty and no one can write books with cold toes.

ABOUT THE AUTHOR

Katie is a human being who lives by the sea in Hove with her husband and two 'lively' sons.

Here is a picture of her at her happiest, dreaming about gin and bunny rabbits, which are two of her favourite things.

hurrahforgin.com
facebook.com/hurrahforgin
Instagram and twitter – @hurrahforgin